JOHN GILCHRIST'S
Cheap Eats
Calgary

Red Deer Press

Copyright © 2002 John Gilchrist

The Publishers
Red Deer Press
813 MacKimmie Library Tower
2500 University Drive NW
Calgary Alberta Canada T2N 1N4
www.reddeerpress.com

Credits
Cover design by Boldface Technologies
Text design by Dennis Johnson
Cover photo courtesy of P. Crowther and S. Carter/Tony Stone Images
Printed and bound in Canada by Friesens for Red Deer Press

Acknowledgments
Financial support provided by the Department of Canadian Heritage, the Alberta Foundation for the Arts, a beneficiary of the Lottery Fund of the Government of Alberta, and the University of Calgary.

National Library of Canada Cataloguing in Publication Data
Main entry under title:
Cheap eats Calgary
ISBN 0-88995-255-8
1. Restaurants—Alberta—Calgary—Guidebooks. 2. Calgary (Alta.)—
Guidebooks. I. Gilchrist, John, 1953–
TX907.5.C22C3 2002   647.957123'38   C2002-910291-X

5 4 3 2 1

Contents

Dedicated to all of those who search out fine food at a great price. Let's eat!

Introduction

Here's a little secret: Every once in a while we local food writers get together for lunch and talk about (guess what?) food! But not just about the latest, greatest, most expensive places. No. We talk about our newest finds—the cheap and cheesy joints where good food is also inexpensive, where the decor may be out of a garage sale and no one has ever worn a tuxedo, but where the charm alone almost makes the visit worthwhile. We love sharing our bargain finds with each other. And here, in this book, I've put together a collection of my favorite cheap eats.

I've been chomping my way around Calgary and the Bow Valley for over two decades now, and I'm continually surprised and pleased with the quality and value of the food available here. There's great ethnic diversity—from Vietnamese noodle houses to Dutch pancake houses to classic Calgarian diners. From old-timers such as Peter's Drive In to new arrivals such as Dawat, each restaurant in this book adds something to the culinary fabric of our area.

I hope my selections prove that cheap food doesn't mean bad food. It's surprising just what kind of value, quality and taste you can find out there. Take, for example, the multi-course lunch at Taketomi Village for $6.75—I'd be impressed at twice the price. And the tasty burritos, quesadillas and chimichangas at Berryhill Tamales and Tacos. There are healthy vegetarian offerings at the Restaurant Indonesia, Saigon and Marathon. Plus the smoothies at Juiced and Core. Good stuff and healthy too.

Not to say that my favorites don't include a number of high fat burger and fries joints. Those definitely thrive, and I have included the better ones plus Calgary's longest-standing fried chicken outlet. Nobody's pretending that they are healthy, but once in a while, it feels good to top up the cholesterol.

You'll meet some interesting characters through this book too. There's the Spoletini brothers (and Mike Palumbo), who've created a mini sausage empire in Inglewood, Jim Rockford who spends his days pumping out great burgers from his burger bus, and Dany

Lamote, who left the world of high-end dining at places like Teatro and The Ranche to make some of the best sandwiches I've ever tasted. There are recent immigrants cooking the food of their homeland, Newfoundland expatriates brewing a fine cup of tea and a bike dealer who always wanted a biker diner.

This book contains 102 recommended restaurants, in 141 locations, to get a tasty lunch for under $10 and dinner for under $15. Some are paper-plates-in-a-food-court places, others are quick drive-ups (or drive-throughs), while others are just high-value sit-down places with great food and excellent service.

As in all my restaurant guides, no one has paid to be included. My selections are based on how well restaurants do their job and how strong the value for the dollar is. I have tried to avoid the big chains not because some of them don't rate inclusion, but rather because they're household words already. Mostly, I have stuck to smaller independents, trying to point out the real gems—both well known and not so well known—that keep my wife, Catherine, and I coming back again and again.

So enjoy. And please let me know if you find other great cheap eating out there that will help me keep up my end of the conversation the next time I get together with other local food writers. Contact me at escurial@cadvision.com.

A&A Foods and Deli

1401 – 20 Avenue NW

Lebanese Fast Food

TELEPHONE
289-1400

HOURS
Monday – Friday
8 AM – 10 PM
Saturday
9 AM – 10 PM
Sunday
9 AM – 9 PM

RESERVATIONS
Not accepted

BEVERAGES
Nonalcoholic only

CARDS
Cash, Debit

Nonsmoking
Takeout & delivery
6 outdoor tables

One day back in the early 1990s, John Bahay was a little bored. Things were slow in his Capitol Hill convenience store, so he started cooking some of the food of his Lebanese homeland. He brought in an upright donair spit roaster, stacked on some fresh, boneless chicken, whipped up some tabouleh and started serving pitas stuffed with hot chicken, falafel or beef. Now, almost 10 years later, he can barely keep up with demand.

On nice days the few outside tables are packed with A&A fans, and there's often a line-up out the door. Inside, Bahay, his cousin Jamal, and various staff and family members churn out the donairs along with a patter that alone is worth the price of admission. Each donair comes with at least three laughs, and the entertainment is as good as the food.

A&A is also a good place to stock up on fig marmalade, Turkish coffee, apricot paste and other Middle Eastern goodies you've been looking for.

Warning: Do not eat an A&A donair while driving—it's a two-hander.

Aida's

2208 – 4 Street SW

Lebanese

TELEPHONE
541-1189

HOURS
Monday
11 AM – 9 PM
Tuesday – Thursday
11 AM – 10 PM
Friday & Saturday
11 AM – 11 PM
Sunday
4 PM – 9 PM

RESERVATIONS
Recommended

BEVERAGES
Fully licensed

CARDS
Visa, MasterCard,
American Express, Debit

Nonsmoking
Takeout & catering

Aida's sits on a busy stretch of 4 Street, but it can be hard to find. Its street presence is minimal, but inside, it is open and airy, seating forty-four under a gold-painted tin ceiling.

The food is very good Lebanese cuisine, fresh and in tune with the current move to lighter, healthier and tastier foods. The fattoush is a crunchy salad of romaine, cucumbers, tomatoes, radishes and pita chips in a sumak and olive oil dressing; a small portion costs $3.95 and a large, only $4.95. Platters of lamb kebabs, falafel or shawarma include fattoush or tabouleh (the parsley and bulgar salad) and hommous or baba ghannouj dips for $7.95. One of my favorite dishes is the mouhammara, a spread of roasted red peppers, walnuts and bread that is wonderfully rich and flavorful on pita.

I like Aida's. In fact, the combination of food, service and value is such that I named it the best new restaurant of 2000.

Alberta King of Subs

7196 Temple Drive NE

Montreal-Style Deli

TELEPHONE
293-5809

HOURS
Monday – Wednesday
10 AM – 9 PM
Thursday – Saturday
10 AM – 10 PM
Sunday
11 AM – 9 PM

RESERVATIONS
Accepted

BEVERAGES
Fully Licensed

CARDS
Visa, Debit

Nonsmoking
Takeout & delivery

Many transplanted Montrealers bemoan the lack of good smoked meat delis outside La Belle Province. The complaints have been long and loud enough that some people around Calgary have tried to alleviate the problem. One of the best efforts is Alberta King of Subs, a nondescript cafe in the Northeast.

Alberta King of Subs looks like a basic, plastic-coated industrial cafe, but the products are as Montreal as they come: hand-cut smoked meat, poutine with Quebec cheese curds, Spruce Beer, Mrs. White's pickles. The smoked meat is layered into subs and sandwiches that top out just under $9—a lot less than a round-trip ticket to Montreal.

The sandwiches are well made too. The staff understand the unique obsession with the perfect smoked meat sandwich and will prepare it any way you like. And with poutine gravy made with juices from the smoked meat, it doesn't get any more authentic.

Annie's

15979 Bow Bottom Trail SE, Bow Valley Ranch

Bakery Cafe

TELEPHONE
225-3920

HOURS
Easter weekend –
Labour Day
Daily 9 AM – 6 PM

RESERVATIONS
Not accepted

BEVERAGES
Nonalcoholic only

CARDS
Visa, MasterCard,
American Express,
Diners Club, Debit

Nonsmoking
Takeout
Porches

Strolling—or biking or blading—through Fish Creek Park can work up an appetite. So many folks drop in to The Ranche—the lovingly restored three-story brick house near Bow Bottom Trail—to pick up a snack. They take a quick look at the menu and see elk rib eyes for $34 and wonder if they shouldn't have dressed a little better. Then they head over to the cute little wood house a couple of hundred meters west for a sandwich and an ice cream cone.

This is Annie's, the former foreman's house at the Bow Valley Ranch and now the more casual adjunct to The Ranche. Annie's is quaint. You can sit on the porch and watch deer grazing a few meters away, and most of the food is made in The Ranche's kitchen. So it's good, hearty, wholesome but a whole lot cheaper.

And at Annie's, there are water bowls outside for your dog. Now how many restaurants offer that.

Anpurna

175 – 52 Street SE

Indian (Vegetarian Gujarati)

TELEPHONE
235-6028

HOURS
Tuesday – Friday
11 AM – 2:30 PM;
5 PM – 8:30 PM
Saturday & Sunday
11 AM – 8:30 PM

RESERVATIONS
Accepted

BEVERAGES
Beer & wine

CARDS
Visa

Nonsmoking
Takeout

Calgary offers a wealth of good Indian restaurants, but only the Anpurna serves the vegetarian cuisine of the province of Gujarat. Tucked into an obscure strip mall on the southwest corner of 52 Street and Memorial Drive SE, the Anpurna's location is almost as unique as its food.

Serious Indian food fans and vegetarians flock to the Anpurna for its chloe puri (chickpea/onion curry), the masala dossa (spiced onions and potatoes in an Indian crepe) and the kachori stuffed with spiced lentils and coconut. A meal here makes one forget that there is no meat on the menu. Note: Dairy products are used.

Popularity has driven up the prices at the Anpurna. The chloe puri has broken through the $5 barrier, and the kachori now scrape against the $4 mark. There's even a mega-meal thali of two curries, dal, rice, roti, dessert, papadum and pickles for $9.95. (At lunch it's $6.95.) Superb value.

Bad Ass Jack's

10233 Elbow Drive SW

20 Crowfoot Crescent NW

TELEPHONE
Elbow Drive
258-2928
Crowfoot Crescent
241-2201

WEB SITE
www.badassjacks.com

HOURS
Elbow Drive
Monday – Saturday
11 AM – 9 PM (till 10 PM
in summer)
Sunday
Noon – 8 PM
Crowfoot Crescent
Monday – Saturday
11 AM – 10 PM
Sunday
11 AM – 8 PM

RESERVATIONS
Not accepted

BEVERAGES
Nonalcoholic only

CARDS
Visa, MasterCard,
American Express, Debit

Nonsmoking
Takeout

Ever wanted to top a falafel sandwich with a Caribbean jerk sauce? Ever been interested in a teriyaki ham and Swiss cheese sub or a meat-loaf sandwich with provolone and peanut sauce? These may sound like odd combinations (and they are), but you can have your food any way you want at Bad Ass Jack's.

There are three Bad Ass Jack's in Calgary, serving up fresh, hot sandwiches and wraps along with rice bowls and cold wraps. Their big claim to fame—aside from those wacky combos—is house-roasted meats and home-made buns. So they carve the beef or chicken right off the roast, making a pretty darn good sandwich. Then they load it up with whatever vegetables (peppers, corn, celery, cabbage, water chestnuts, etc.) you'd like and sauce. With almost everything under $7, Bad Ass Jack's gives you a lot of food for the money. Everything is fresh, and, with some imagination, you can put together some unforgettable flavors.

Bagolac

6130 – 1A Street SW

Vietnamese & Thai

TELEPHONE
252-5588

HOURS
Monday – Thursday
11 AM – 9 PM
Friday & Saturday
11 AM – 10 PM
Call ahead if arriving late
in the evening.

RESERVATIONS
Not accepted

BEVERAGES
Fully licensed

CARDS
Visa, MasterCard,
American Express, Debit

Nonsmoking
Takeout

At any given lunch hour, the small waiting area at the front of the Bagolac is packed with folks waiting for their turn at a bowl of Vietnamese bun. All 150 seats are usually filled before noon on a first-come, first-served basis.

Bagolac is big favorite of the firefighters and police officers who work nearby. The small tables are always packed with people in uniform slurping back noodles and rice in their various forms. Bagolac offers 159 items on the menu, many of them meals in themselves and all but two under $10. Most folks seem to order the big bowls of noodles, broth, greens and meat known as bun—at a typical lunch over 200 portions of the stuff are served. And with the bun ranging from $6 – $9, it makes a nice lunch that doesn't lighten the wallet or weigh you down for the afternoon.

Service is crisp and swift; dishes appear within seconds of ordering. My personal record is lunch in 12 minutes from entering Bagolac to leaving.

Barpa Bill's Souvlaki

223 Bear Street, Banff

Greek Fast Food

TELEPHONE
403-762-0377

HOURS
Daily 11 AM – 9 PM

RESERVATIONS
Not accepted

BEVERAGES
Nonalcoholic only

CARDS
Visa

Nonsmoking
Takeout & catering

I know, I know. This is a book about great cheap places to eat in Calgary. But we have to hit the mountains once in a while, don't we? And do we really want to pay Banff prices? (Well, sure. If someone else is picking up the tab, let's head to the Banffshire Club or Le Beaujolais or The Pines.) But hunger awaits at high altitude, and there's no one better to knock it off at a good price than Barpa Bill. (That's Uncle Bill to the non-Greeks out there.)

Barpa Bill's is a tiny place (twelve stools, no tables) that serves the best souvlaki this side of Athens. They fire up skewered meats, fold them into outstanding pita imported from Chicago, plop in tomatoes and lettuce, and lace the whole thing with a breath-wrenching, garlic tzatziki sauce. People will grant you a wide berth after one of these babies.

Bill's also does a mean spinach pie, great stuffed vine leaves and even some burgers. And almost nothing is over $5. That's great value anywhere, let alone in downtown Banff.

Berryhill Tamales and Tacos

200 Barclay Parade (Eau Claire Market)

Mexican

TELEPHONE
262-4677

HOURS
Monday – Friday
11 AM – 11 PM
Saturday
9 AM – 11PM
Sunday
9 AM – 9 PM

RESERVATIONS
Accepted for groups of
12 or more

BEVERAGES
Fully licensed

CARDS
Visa, MasterCard,
American Express, Debit

Non-smoking section
Take-out & catering

For over forty years Walter Berryhill sold tamales out of a push cart in downtown Houston. In the competitive world of Texas street tamales, Berryhill distinguished himself by wearing a top hat and using a white corn meal instead of the traditional corn masa for his tamales. He also created a chili gravy that was poured over his lard-laden tamales, making them irresistible.

After Berryhill's retirement, a Texas lawyer bought his recipes, and eventually a small chain of restaurants was built in Houston producing tamales and another Gulf Coast specialty—fish tacos. And in the chilly spring of 2002, the first Canadian Berryhill opened in Calgary.

It's large space done in bright Mexican colours, filled with Spanish-speaking staff. There's a fresh salsa bar, house-squeezed lime margaritas and an initially confusing ordering system. Once sorted out, the food arrives hot and fast and with enough kick to satisfy most chili heads. The menu includes a variety of burritos, quesadillas and chimichangas, plus a list of Mexican breakfast dishes.

Bisque au Tech

630 – 3 Avenue SW (Shaw Court)

Bakery Cafe

TELEPHONE
232-0277

HOURS
Monday – Friday
7:30 AM – 3:30 PM

RESERVATIONS
Not accepted

BEVERAGES
Nonalcoholic only

CARDS
Cash only

Nonsmoking
Takeout

Most downtown office complexes have some sort of quick and easy food outlet. It may be a chain restaurant or a corporate cafeteria, but few are elevated to the level of the Bisque au Tech in Shaw Court.

Run by former Savoir Fare partner Peter Fraiberg, Bisque au Tech does the soup and sandwich bit with flare and substance. The chicken club has real chicken breast with crisp bacon on a house-made roll; the cream of vegetable soup would cost a lot more served in a china bowl in fancier places; the peanut butter brownie is a bizarre combination that makes me want to run back for one right now. Soup, sandwich and a drink will run well under $10. Daily specials are even cheaper.

Bisque au Tech occupies a spacious lobby that is filled each day with Shaw workers relaxing and playing cards, chatting or watching the huge wall of televisions. This is the way a corporate cafe should be. And on top of that, it is fully open to the public.

Black Bull

53 Hunterhorn Road NE

Pub

TELEPHONE
274-2855

HOURS
Monday – Saturday
11 AM – 2 AM
Sunday
11 AM – midnight

RESERVATIONS
Accepted

BEVERAGES
Fully licensed

CARDS
Visa, MasterCard,
American Express, Debit

No nonsmoking section
Takeout

If you like a room with a brew (and a cloud of smoke) and you're in the northern reaches of Calgary, Black Bull may be your kind of place. Just be forewarned that this is one of the smokiest places in this book. It's almost too smoky to appreciate what is really some pretty good pub food. But then again, it is a multi-TV, dartboard, pool table kinda pub, where every table is outfitted with an ashtray.

Black Bull does the cross-cultural pub style of shepherd's pie and meat loaf, fish and chips, and burgers with almost everything on the menu under $10. The quintuple-decker sandwich cleans out the fridge with layers of crisp bacon, roast beef and turkey, cheeses and greens on white bread (sorry, no brown). It has to be disassembled to eat, unless you have a more flexible jaw than I do.

This is *big* food done reasonably well with a fast kitchen and friendly pub service. They appear to take their food as seriously as their beer and, unfortunately, their tobacco.

Blue Nile

322 – 10 Street NW

Ethiopian

TELEPHONE
270-4550

HOURS
Daily 11:30 AM – 11 PM

RESERVATIONS
Accepted

BEVERAGES
Fully licensed

CARDS
Visa, American Express,
Diners Club, Debit

Nonsmoking
Takeout

Blue Nile is the most recent of the few Ethiopian restaurants to arrive in Calgary— and already it has moved. It started in a small house on the west side of 10 Street NW, but when the building was demolished, it managed to move right across the street. The bright new space seats about forty and offers a bigger kitchen to work in.

The tables are topped with colorfully woven messobs, the covered serving containers used in Ethiopia. The food is typically served on a flat, crepy bread called injera, which lays on a tray inside the messob. The food is then scooped up by hand using the injera. No cutlery is needed because the food is mostly cooked in wats or stews.

The best way to sample Blue Nile's food is at the lunch buffet ($7.50), where four vegetarian and four meat dishes and endless injera are offered. The flavors are rich and deep; there's nothing else quite like it.

Boogie's Burgers

908 Edmonton Trail NE

Hamburgers

TELEPHONE
230-7070

HOURS
Monday – Saturday
10 AM – 10 PM

RESERVATIONS
Accepted

BEVERAGES
Beer & wine

CARDS
Cash only

Nonsmoking section
Takeout
1 table outside

You want character in a restaurant along with high value? How about Boogie's Burgers, a thirty-year-old burger shack on Edmonton Trail. It was started by a couple from Paris and was one of the very few places in Calgary to offer espresso and citron pressé with their burgers. Wait, make that the only place.

Late in 2000 the original couple retired (back to Paris, sigh) selling Boogie's to a South African family—father John, son Keith and daughter Noelle. Thankfully the menu hasn't changed much. You can still get a Super-Faye burger named after one of the original owners, the spicy fries and that espresso. The prices remain well within reason, with the biggest burger under $7, and the service is as personal and professional as ever.

Boogie's was expanded before the transition and now has distinct smoking and nonsmoking sections and a short alcohol list. That just makes dining on one of the city's best burgers all the more comfortable.

Burger Inn

9669 Macleod Trail SW

920 – 36 Street NE

3829 Bow Trail SW

2020 – 4 Street SW (Watch for opening)

128 Edmonton Trail, Airdrie

Hamburgers

TELEPHONE
Macleod Trail
252-4840
36 Street
235-5860
Bow Trail
685-0825
4 Street
244-9293
Edmonton Trail
912-0369

HOURS
Monday – Saturday
11 AM – 10 PM
(Edmonton Trail till 9 PM)
Sunday & holidays
Noon – 9 PM

RESERVATIONS
Accepted

BEVERAGES
Nonalcoholic only

CARDS
Visa, MasterCard,
American Express, Debit

Nonsmoking
Takeout

Ever wanted to try an ostrich burger? How about venison or buffalo? Or just a good old cheeseburger with some hand-cut, freshly dipped fries? Burger Inn is a small burger empire of five stores that does its burgering the old-fashioned way—one at a time when they are ordered.

The Burger Inns have made a name for themselves with their exotic meat burgers, but a quick survey of their customers—many self-proclaimed burger buffs—shows that most just like a good super half-pounder for $5. (That's two big patties with cheese.) A single burger is a decent $2.39 and is often matched up with fries and a pop for a value packed $3.97. A spicier burger called the B.I.G. is also a hot seller as are the usual burger mates of onion rings and shakes.

The surroundings are utilitarian and ordering is done at the counter. Service consists of staff shouting out the type of burger hot off the grill and seeing how many people respond.

Cafe de Tokyo

630 – 1 Avenue NE

Japanese

TELEPHONE
264-2027

HOURS
Monday – Friday
11:30 AM – 2:30 PM,
5 PM – 9 PM
Saturday
Noon – 9 PM

RESERVATIONS
Accepted

BEVERAGES
Beer, sake & wine

CARDS
Cash only

Nonsmoking
Takeout

The Cafe de Tokyo stands out not only as a great-value eatery but also as the best of the small collection of Japanese noodle shops around town. Most Japanese restaurants focus on the sushi side of things (and, in fact, the Cafe de Tokyo does do sushi), but the real reason to visit this Bridgeland cafe is for the ramen noodle soups.

The soups feature handmade stocks, perfectly cooked noodles, delicate toppings of pork and chicken, and gyoza dumplings, all put together by skilled and experienced Japanese chef Ken Doshida.

It's a good thing that the food is tasty and cheap because the atmosphere is nothing to write home about. The vinyl chairs are in need of repair, the smoking section clogs any fresh air and it's just plain crowded. But it is also very humid with all the stock pots boiling away making it a great place to visit on a cold and dry winter's evening.

Cafe Metro

7400 Macleod Trail SW

112 – 4 Avenue SW (Sun Life Plaza)

Montreal-Style Bistro

TELEPHONE
Macleod Trail
255-6537
Sun Life Plaza
233-0777

HOURS
Macleod Trail
Sunday – Thursday
11 AM – 9 PM
Friday
11 AM – 10 PM
Saturday
11 AM – 10 PM
Sun Life Plaza
Monday – Friday
7 AM – 3 PM
Saturday
11 AM – 10 PM

RESERVATIONS
Accepted for groups of
six or more

BEVERAGES
Fully licensed

CARDS
Visa, MasterCard,
American Express, Debit

Nonsmoking section
Takeout

Outside, the Cafe Metro looks like a bay in any Macleod Trail strip mall. Inside, it's a delightfully over-the-top Montreal street scene complete with streetlights, hanging laundry and fire hydrants—out of place for Macleod Trail but quite in keeping with the smoked meat sandwiches available here. Fortunately, the tables are more widely spaced and the air is less smoky than the Montreal cafes.

Cafe Metro serves Delstar smoked meat on rye with mustard for $8.25 and mega sizes with 50% more meat for $9.95. They also do a Reuben, a Philly beef with Swiss cheese, a Monte Cristo and a chicken club, all well under $10. Plus, there are burgers, pasta, pizza and steaks, but the sandwiches are what draw people back time and again—that and the funky surroundings.

In 2001, Cafe Metro opened a second location in the food court at Sun Life Plaza for those not wanting to make the trek south.

Caffe Beano

1613 – 9 Street SW

Coffee House

TELEPHONE
229-1232

HOURS
Daily 6 AM – midnight

RESERVATIONS
Not accepted

BEVERAGES
Nonalcoholic only

CARDS
Cash only

Nonsmoking
Takeout
Outdoor benches
(smoking)

Owned and operated by the charmingly energetic Rhonda Siebens, Caffe Beano is one of the best coffee houses in the city. It's not because of the tight and confusing ordering area or the cramped tables or the often deafening acoustics. It's because, in spite of these drawbacks, people enjoy working at Beano, and customers like hanging out there. Sure, the coffee is good, the sandwiches are tasty and the muffins are hands down the best in town. But what many people find irresistible about the place is its positive energy. On any given day, you will find a cross section of clientele from Beamer-driving yuppies to laptop writers to retirees from Mount Royal.

Beano's big consumable draw is the rich, dark coffee, but the house-made sandwiches have proven to be a big hit too with a bundle of good ingredients for $4.75. Those heavy muffins go perfectly with the coffee and, at $1.25, are more than worth it for the weight alone.

Calgary Sweet House

5320 – 8 Avenue SE

Indian Bakery

TELEPHONE
272-7234

HOURS
Wednesday – Monday
9 AM – 8:30 PM

RESERVATIONS
Accepted

BEVERAGES
Nonalcoholic only

CARDS
Visa, MasterCard, Diners
Club, Debit

Nonsmoking
Takeout, delivery &
catering

For over 20 years the Calgary Sweet House has been producing some of the best jalebis, burfi and rasmalai in the city. For the uninitiated, those are just interesting words; for fans of super-sweet Indian desserts, they are an almost daily necessity.

The Sweet House hasn't changed a lot in the last two decades. It's a high-ceilinged, rectangular room that could double as any industrial cafeteria with its red vinyl chairs, rows of tables and a cooler in the corner. The key distinction is in the long display counter that holds all the sweet delights from brightly colored jalebis to bins of seasoned nuts. Available in single slices or by the pound, choices are plentiful.

The Sweet House also does full meals with curried goat, tandoori chicken and paneer with naan, all under $8. And a good (Styrofoam) cup of chai masala is only $1. The Sweet House may not be stylish, but it is sweet—and cheap.

Chicken-On-The-Way

1443 Kensington Road NW

Chicken

TELEPHONE
283-5545

HOURS
Monday – Thursday
10:30 AM – 12:30 AM
Friday & Saturday
10:30 AM – 1:30 AM
Sunday
10:30 AM – 11 PM

RESERVATIONS
Not accepted

BEVERAGES
Nonalcoholic only

CARDS
Visa

Nonsmoking
Takeout & delivery
Outdoor tables

A lot of chickens have died in the service of Chicken-On-The-Way over the last forty-three years. That's how long this Hillhurst landmark has been serving their special brand of fried chicken at the corner of 14 Street and Kensington Road NW.

Moderate diners line up for the 3-Piece Dinner, which features (of course) three pieces of chicken, fries, gravy or slaw, and one of the house specialties—a corn fritter—for $5.85. Famished diners load up on the Hungry Man Dinner, which adds two pieces of chicken and an extra fritter for $7.95. If you want to go exotic, the shrimp dinner is $8.

But don't go expecting a burger at Chicken-On-The-Way. It's chicken first and forever, served in the distinctive yellowish boxes that impart a pulpy aroma that is part of the overall flavor. And that's just the way the regulars want it. It's an addiction for some, a reward for others, a ritual for even more. It's Chicken-On-The-Way, and thankfully it never changes.

Chico's Tecate Grill

3168 Sunridge Boulevard NE

Cal-Mex

TELEPHONE
250-1112

HOURS
Monday – Friday
11 AM – 9 PM

RESERVATIONS
Accepted

BEVERAGES
Beer, wine & margaritas

CARDS
Visa, MasterCard,
American Express, Debit

Nonsmoking section
Takeout
Patio (smoking)

Chico's Tecate Grill is the only Canadian outlet of a small California–Mexican chain based in the southern California farming community of Temecula. (The other two international locations are Cairo and Amsterdam. Go figure.)

This could easily be just another bland taco stand but for the fact that Chico's makes all their salsas fresh daily. And they are well made. The pico de gallo is fresh and light, the tomatillo-based salsa verde has a mild, savory flavor, the picosa is a robust rendition, the casera bites back and the roasted pasilla is darned good. These are salsas that other places pretend to serve and rarely do; the only complaint Chico's ever receives about its salsas is from people who think their salsas should be even hotter.

What the sauces go with is pretty good too. The chicken is marinated, then chopped and folded into tortillas and served with rice and beans for $9.69; the bean burrito loads a meal onto a plate in under $5. Chico's is not the prettiest food in the world, but it's fresh, tasty and packs a chili punch.

Chili Club

555 – 11 Avenue SW

Thai

TELEPHONE
237-8828

HOURS
Monday – Friday
11:30 AM – 2 PM
Tuesday – Sunday
5 PM – 10 PM

RESERVATIONS
Recommended

BEVERAGES
Fully licensed

CARDS
Visa, MasterCard,
American Express,
Debit, Diners Club

Nonsmoking
Takeout & delivery

In the early 1990s, the Chili Club was the hottest restaurant in town, literally and figuratively. It burned brightly for a brief period, then disappeared. But after a few years, the concept was revived, and, with the same chef, the restaurant reopened.

It's a lovely room drenched in deep reds with gold highlights. The setting works perfectly with a menu than runs from panang duck curry and Phad Prig Khing Gai (chicken with string beans) to Tom Yum soup and Yum Nuer salad. Some of the dishes push into the mid-teens, but it is still possible to have a nice meal at the Chili Club for under $15 (under $10 if you stick to the noodles and soups).

Heat is designated by one, two or three chilis; they are not shy about stoking the flames in this food, so be careful if that's your concern.

Chuckwagon Cafe

105 Sunset Boulevard SW, Turner Valley

Breakfast

TELEPHONE
933-0003

HOURS
Monday – Friday
7 AM – 3 PM
Saturday
7 AM – 4 PM
Sunday
8 AM – 4 PM

RESERVATIONS
Not accepted

BEVERAGES
Nonalcoholic only

CARDS
Cash only

Nonsmoking section
Takeout
Patio

If you're rambling into the foothills south of the city, all that fresh air can build up an appetite. And if you haven't packed a lunch, the vittles can get a bit sparse. But one place that has city and country folk alike lining up for chow is the Chuckwagon Cafe in Turner Valley.

Situated on the colorfully named Sunset Boulevard, the Chuckwagon is a little red barn that has a rustic wood and western interior. It's divided into two sections—smoking and non—with the kitchen and an ice cream counter in the middle.

The Chuckwagon does the bacon and egg, huevos rancheros and breakfast burrito-style of breakfast dining well. The servings are huge, the service is fast and the cup of coffee is bottomless, and the Ranchman's breakfast is the priciest item at $8.25. For that you get a belly-stretching three eggs, ham, sausage, bacon, toast, hashbrowns and fruit salad. Big meal and decent quality too.

Clay Oven

3132 – 26 Street NE (Interpacific Business Park)

Indian (Punjabi)

TELEPHONE
250-2161

HOURS
Monday – Friday
11:30 AM – 2 PM,
5 PM – 10 PM
Saturday
5 PM – 10 PM

RESERVATIONS
Recommended

BEVERAGES
Fully licensed

CARDS
Visa, American Express,
Debit

Nonsmoking
Takeout

Some Indian food fans love the tandoori-roasted meats. Some go for the rich vegetarian dishes. And still others love the breads—the thick doughy naan, the buttery paratha and the thin, tasty chapati. For those of the breadish persuasion, the Clay Oven is *the* place.

Every time I visit the Clay Oven, I am impressed by the breads. But they do not stand alone. The lamb vindaloo is hot and tangy, the chicken tikka is beautifully prepared, and the daal and paneer dishes are excellent.

Dinner here can be pricey, with most dishes ranging from $8 – $12 (still very good value), so the most economical way to sample the Clay Oven is at their buffet lunch. For only $9 you can sample a wide array of their work.

The Clay Oven is small but well maintained, and the service is always pleasant. It can be tricky to find in the Interpacific Business Park. Just look for the big Canadian flag at the Husky Truckstop on Barlow and 32 Avenue NE. The Clay Oven is just to the east of that.

Core Cafe

105A Stephen Avenue Walk SW

Cafe & Juice Bar

TELEPHONE
263-2673

HOURS
Monday – Tuesday
7 AM – 5 PM
Wednesday – Friday
7 AM – 7 PM
Saturday
10 AM – 4 PM
Sunday
12 AM – 4 PM
Varies seasonally

RESERVATIONS
Accepted

BEVERAGES
Beer & wine (license pending)

CARDS
Visa, American Express, Debit

Nonsmoking
Takeout & delivery
Patio

Core Cafe sits like the quiet cousin on a block of high-powered restaurants. But, because it focuses on fresh, light, local, healthy (even some vegan) cuisine, Core is packed most days. It doesn't hurt that the pita wrap Montreal smoked meat sandwich, the bean and basil salad, and the blueberry-strawberry-saskatoon smoothie are each under $5. It's good stuff too. The idea of healthy food translates into tasty these days.

Core also does some very nice baking (the blueberry bran muffins are excellent), and there's always some kind of gooey loaf that goes well with the smoothies.

The decor is a nice change from many downtown eateries too. They have used the long, narrow space well, exposing the historic stones walls and splashing soft light onto them. It's a comfortable place for lunch, as light on the wallet as it is on the stomach. And for those working nearby, Core Cafe can deliver affordable catered lunches too.

Crazyweed Kitchen

626 – 8 Street, Canmore

Global Cuisine

TELEPHONE
609-2530

HOURS
Daily 11 AM – 7 PM

RESERVATIONS
Not accepted

BEVERAGES
Nonalcoholic only

CARDS
Visa, MasterCard, Debit

Nonsmoking
Takeout & catering
4 outdoor tables

Crazyweed represents not only the best value for food in Canmore, but the best food—bar none—in this book. It is a funky little place with only a few tables (and those are outside) and some of the best food you will find anywhere.

Sure, you can spent a whack of bucks here if you're going for the scallops or the veal chops, but if you stick to the small, regular menu of burgers and lamb sandwiches, or if you select from the display counter filled with various salads and vegetarian options, you can stuff yourself for under $10.

If you're lucky you may get a seat at one of the fourteen stools pushed up against a counter laden with the latest interesting magazines. Or you may have to tote your food away. In either case you'll be happy. Crazyweed is one of the very few places I've ever been where the food brought tears to my eyes because it was so good.

Crete Souvlaki

2623 – 17 Avenue SW

Greek Fast Food

TELEPHONE
246-4777

HOURS
Monday – Friday
9 AM – 10 PM
Saturday & Sunday
11:30 AM – 9:30 PM

RESERVATIONS
Not accepted

BEVERAGES
Nonalcoholic only

CARDS
Visa, MasterCard,
American Express, Debit

Nonsmoking
Takeout

The combination of fast gas and fast food is unbeatable—especially if the food is of decent quality. (I'm not talking about those microwaved mysteries found in most gas station stores.) The Crete Souvlaki takes up about 50% of a busy 17 Avenue OK Gas & Convenience Store and whips out fresh souvlaki, hommous and horiatiki at a brisk pace.

Alternating between whiffs of garlic and gasoline, patrons belly up to the counter (with a view of the pumps!) or slide into the two tables beside the auto supplies. It's not pretty, but the most expensive item on the menu is the lamb souvlaki with Greek salad for $6. (Oops! I forgot the moussaka with salad for $8.25). You're not going to find quite the same caliber of food as, say, at the Santorini Taverna, but it's fresh, filling and you get your windows washed.

And true to the pit stop style, you can have both your tank and your stomach filled in under twenty minutes.

Dawat

517 – 10 Avenue SW

Indian (Punjabi)

TELEPHONE
269-4700

HOURS
Daily 11:30 AM – 2 PM,
5 PM – 10 PM

RESERVATIONS
Recommended for lunch

BEVERAGES
Fully licensed

CARDS
Visa, MasterCard,
American Express, Debit

Nonsmoking
Takeout, delivery &
catering

Just under the railroad tracks from the downtown core, the Dawat sits in a tiny strip mall on the corner of 4 Street and 10 Avenue SW. It's a short walk for some very fine Punjabi cuisine. (Note: For non-downtowners, there is parking in front. Just plug the pay station, bring in your ticket stub and you will be reimbursed. Now there's a big plus!)

Sisters Sarbjit and Manjit are running their own place now after cooking at the Taj Mahal for many years. Dawat is an unassuming forty-seater that fills daily with buffeters tucking into a thirty-five-item Punjabi lunch for a reasonable $9.95. The mix changes frequently, but you will likely find tandoori chicken, mutter paneer, pakoras of various kinds and a range of curries.

Ordering off the menu can get pricier, with an order of lamb kebabs coming in at $20, but many of the other dishes—especially the lengthy list of vegetarian offerings—stay well under $10. Very reasonable for the quality, the setting and the fine service.

Dieu's Wok

7204 Fairmount Drive SE

Chinese (Szechwan & Peking)

TELEPHONE
252-8025

HOURS
Sunday – Thursday
4 PM – 11 PM
Friday & Saturday
4 PM – 1 AM

RESERVATIONS
Not accepted

BEVERAGES
Nonalcoholic only

CARDS
Visa, MasterCard, Debit

Nonsmoking
Takeout, delivery &
catering

Dieu's Wok is one of those nondescript places that drops menus in your mailbox on a regular basis. The menus contain the usual Chinese favorites—ginger beef, grilled dumplings, salt-and-pepper shrimp. Most of these places are pretty ordinary.

However, Dieu's Wok stands out for its quality. The ingredients at this tiny Fairview takeout joint are quite good. And the preparation and saucing elevates it far beyond the containers it comes in. The Singapore noodles for $7 bite back in a bright curry that doesn't inundate the well-cooked noodles. The fried noodles with three different seafoods show a different style with a deeply flavored sauce balancing the flavors of the seafood.

Dieu's Wok is still a takeout place that is first and foremost fast and cheap, with only a couple of dishes breaking $10, but you can tell that care is taken in preparing the food. Perhaps it's because all they do is takeout, and they don't have to worry about table service.

Diner Deluxe

804 Edmonton Trail NE

Diner

TELEPHONE
276-5499

HOURS
Monday
7:30 AM – 4 PM
Tuesday – Friday
7:30 AM – 9 PM
Saturday
8 AM – 9 PM
Sunday
8 AM – 4 PM

RESERVATIONS
Accepted

BEVERAGES
Fully licensed

CARDS
Visa, MasterCard,
American Express,
Diners Club, Debit

Nonsmoking
Takeout
Patio

Many diners have opened in recent years with a variety of retro looks. But none succeeds to the same degree as Diner Deluxe at the crest of Edmonton Trail. Over a year in the building, Diner Deluxe holds the best collection of vintage restaurant wares in the niftiest setting this side of *American Graffiti*.

Vinyl-clad chairs, sweeping space-age lamps, 1950s movie posters and an angular lunch counter fill the space. The attention to detail is superb, with pastel walls and an elevated roof window through which light streams into the room.

The food is the creation of Dwayne and Alberta Ennest, two former denizens of the River Cafe. They have carried over the sensibility of local, organic and fresh wherever possible. The organic barley and beef soup is superb, the bacon and eggs are divine, and the burgers are jaw-widening treats. And there's nothing on the menu over $10. The service is quick and the coffee isn't half bad either.

Dutchie's

3745 Memorial Drive SE (Glencrest Centre)

Caribbean

TELEPHONE
204-8197

HOURS
Monday – Wednesday
11 AM – 8 PM
Thursday – Saturday
11 AM – 11 PM

RESERVATIONS
Accepted

BEVERAGES
Fully licensed

CARDS
Visa, MasterCard,
American Express, Debit

Strictly nonsmoking section
Takeout

In the Caribbean scheme of things, Lloyd's begat Sam's which begat Dutchie's. The big difference is that while there was a Lloyd and a Sam, there is no Dutchie. This little Caribbean cafe on Memorial Drive is currently run by Milton Joseph, a fellow who knows how to do a good jerk chicken and who named the place after a cooking pot rather than himself.

Dutchie's is in a nondescript strip mall space that fills regularly with jerk fiends, brown chicken fans and roti lovers. The spices are heavy here but totally in keeping with their Island heritage. The patties ($1.35 each) are flaky and rich while the brown chicken is a mini-feast at $9. The jerk is hot enough to scorch your tonsils if you're not ready for it.

Dutchie's also comes with the requisite Caribbean drinks and breads, and the air is filled with Island music. And it's one of the very few places around town you can find a good oxtail.

Edelweiss Village

1921 – 20 Avenue NW

German

TELEPHONE
282-6722

HOURS
Monday – Wednesday
9:30 AM – 7 PM
Thursday & Friday
9:30 AM – 8 PM
Saturday
9:30 AM – 6 PM

RESERVATIONS
Accepted for large
groups only

BEVERAGES
Nonalcoholic only

CARDS
Visa, MasterCard, Debit

Nonsmoking
Takeout & catering
Patio

Pound for pound (or calorie for calorie), you probably won't find more food for the dollar than at Edelweiss Village. It is full-force German cuisine with all the wursts and krauts and spaetzle that the culture has to offer.

The Edelweiss Village is a recent arrival to Capitol Hill, a grand expansion on what was once a small Brentwood Mall deli. It has a majestic Bavarian look and enough space to carry all the German (and Dutch, Swiss and Austrian) goodies that expatriates miss. It also has a forty-five-seat cafe and a patio for the overflow.

Regulars order the bratwurst meal with sauerkraut, cabbage and potato salad for $7.50, or they kick it up a notch with the schnitzel at $8.75. Then there's the Village combo, consisting of a cabbage roll, a bratwurst and vegetables for $9.75. To finish off, there are Black Forest cakes for $3.95 a slice or baked cheesecakes for $3.50. And that's not even counting all the cheeses and cold cuts.

Falafel King

803 – 1 Street SW

Mediterranean

TELEPHONE
269-5464

HOURS
Monday – Saturday
11 AM – 9 PM
Sunday
11 AM – 5 PM

RESERVATIONS
Not accepted

BEVERAGES
Nonalcoholic only

CARDS
MasterCard, Debit

Nonsmoking
Takeout & delivery
Patio

Look for the crown and the Falafel King cannot be far behind. The huge golden crown hangs over 1 Street like an old Monarch Margarine ad; inside, the flavors are anything but bland. The Falafel King offers food "as fresh as a Mediterranean breeze," a collection of shawarmas (beef, chicken or mixed), dips (hommous, baba ghannouj), salads (tabouleh, fattoush) and, of course, falafel.

The setup is quite simple with an order-at-the-counter system, a few tables inside and a few more under the protection of the crown. Many folks pop in for quick takeout while others take delivery in their downtown offices.

The Falafel King does it good and fast, and treats his subjects well with nothing over $6 on the menu. You can even wander into the Juice Kingdom for a fresh-squeezed OJ or banana shake, or pick up a King dessert such as baklava. The food is fresh and light, except on the garlic. And the falafel are pretty decent. Long live the King!

Fat Kee

3132 – 26 Street NE (Interpacific Business Park)

CANTONESE &
PEKING/BEIJING

TELEPHONE
250-8436

HOURS
Monday – Saturday
11 AM – 10 PM

RESERVATIONS
Accepted

BEVERAGES
Beer only

CARDS
Visa, MasterCard

Nonsmoking
Takeout & delivery

You want your food fast? Well, then, you'd better know what you want before you sit down at Fat Kee. The staff guide you quickly to your table and are ready to take your order on the way. Regulars roll off numbers such as #82—satay chicken with fried Shanghai noodles—or #91—spareribs in black bean sauce on steamed rice. The staff will linger a moment or two, but then they're off to help someone more decisive. They'll be back—and heaven help you if you aren't ready then.

The food arrives almost as fast in this northeast hole-in-the-wall. The space is actually quite large, but its total lack of atmosphere gives it a hole-in-the-wall feel. It's mostly clean and efficient, with the staff cranked to high gear.

The food is hot and fresh (this place is so busy nothing sits around long) and cheap. An order of spareribs hits $9, but that's for the family size. Seafood dishes creep up to $10, but most items range from $6 – $8. Fast and cheap—just be prepared.

Friends

45 Edenwold Drive NW (Edgepoint Village)

Bakery Cafe

TELEPHONE
241-5526

HOURS
Monday – Thursday
7 AM – 10 PM
Friday
7 AM – 10:30 PM
Saturday
8 AM – 5 PM
Sunday
9 AM – 5 PM

RESERVATIONS
Accepted

BEVERAGES
Fully licensed

CARDS
Visa, MasterCard,
American Express

Nonsmoking
Takeout, delivery &
catering
Patio

It's heartening to find a decent, independent cafe in one of our newer neighborhoods. So much of the restaurant space in the new areas is consumed by cookie-cutter chains. It's also heartening to see a neighborhood independent that is as strongly supported by the community as Friends. This forty-two-seat Edgemont cafe is a gathering place for the neighborhood, a focal point of the community.

And it has the quality to back up the support. Pretty much everything is made on-site — from the grilled focaccia sandwiches of turkey and mozzarella or eggplant and brie ($5.50 – $6.50) to the turtle brownies and confetti squares ($2 – $3). The menu each day offers two soups, such as squash-and-bean or corn chowder ($3.50 – $4.50), plus a soup and sandwich special ($6 – $8) to go along with the eclectic, homey atmosphere.

You won't find Rachel and Ross kanoodling on the couch in this version of Friends, but you will find an active and vital suburban cafe.

Galaxie Diner

1413 – 11 Street SW

Diner

TELEPHONE
228-0001

WEB SITE
www.galaxiediner.com

HOURS
Monday – Friday
7 AM – 3 PM
Saturday, Sunday &
Holidays
8 AM – 4 PM

RESERVATIONS
Not accepted

BEVERAGES
Nonalcoholic only

CARDS
Cash only

Nonsmoking
Takeout

The Galaxie is a tiny, red-vinyl, twirly-stooled diner seating a couple of dozen. It's not a nouveau diner—this stuff is genuine. The napkin dispensers, the stools, even the Kellogg's breakfast cereal display, are all the real thing. An abbreviated lunch counter seats six on those stools, while four vinyl-coated booths pack in another sixteen. In the window nook, two small tables hold another four. It's cozy, with the kitchen consuming the center of the room. Everything has the slightly dented look of a real diner, including the jukeboxes in each booth.

The food also has a legitimate diner taste, all grilled on a stove that protrudes into the dining area. You can watch as they put together breakfast burritos of scrambled eggs, peppers and onions in tortillas or the ever-popular Galaxie burgers layered with cheese, bacon, mushrooms, peppers and onions.

Low fat this is not. But fairly low cost it is, with everything under $6. For the atmosphere and the food, it's a steal—if you can get a seat.

Golden Inn

107 – 2 Avenue SE

Chinese (Cantonese)

TELEPHONE
269-2211

HOURS
Sunday – Thursday
4 PM – 3 AM
Friday & Saturday
4 PM – 4 AM

RESERVATIONS
Accepted

BEVERAGES
Fully licensed

CARDS
Visa, MasterCard,
American Express, Debit

Nonsmoking section
Takeout

The Golden Inn is one of those Chinatown joints where culinary time appears to have stood still. The room is large and characterless, the service impersonal and the style a form of Cantonese that harkens back decades. Yet it remains a classic in its genre.

The food remains good. The Law Ding black-bean chicken is salty, thick with sauce and chunks of chicken and laced with beans and onions. The braised 8 Joe duck incorporates seven other meats with incredibly tender duck breast. And a serving of simple mixed vegetables is a delightful blend of baby corn, broccoli, bok choy and huge mushrooms. Not overly thickened, just lightly sauced.

The Golden Inn also has some of the oddest hours in town. They do no lunch business, preferring to open at 4 PM and to stay open until 3 or 4 AM. Needless to say, the crowd becomes quite interesting after about 2 AM. This is a night owl's hangout and, as such, has the bleary-eyed tone that seems appropriate in the wee hours.

Good Earth

1502 – 11 Street SW

119 Stephen Avenue Walk SW

7007 – 14 Street SW (Rockyview Hospital)

200 Barclay Parade SW (Eau Claire Market)

103A – 1600, 90 Avenue SW (Glenmore Landing)

1403 – 29 Street NW (Foothills Hospital)

616 Macleod Trail South (W.R. Castell Library)

856 Campus Place, 2500 University Drive NW
(ICT Building, U of C; opening soon)

Bakery Cafe

TELEPHONE
11 Street
228-9543
Stephen Avenue Walk
265-2636
Rockyview Hospital
253-5657
Eau Claire Market
237-8684
Glenmore Landing
640-4008
Foothills Hospital
270-4140
W. R. Castell Library
261-2996
ICT Building, U of C
TBA

HOURS
Daily 6:30 AM – 10 PM
(May vary at individual
locations)

RESERVATIONS
Not accepted

BEVERAGES
Beer & wine at Stephen
Avenue location only

CARDS
Visa, Debit

Nonsmoking
Takeout & catering
Patios at 11 Street,
Stephen Avenue, Eau
Claire, Glenmore &
Castell locations

Over the past decade the Good Earth has quietly built itself into a small coffee and baked goods empire with eight locations across Calgary. They seem to thrive in an institutional environment with two locations in hospitals, one in a library, one at the U of C and one in an art gallery. (The Stephen Avenue cafe is in the Art Gallery of Calgary.)

The Good Earth specializes in freshly baked breads and goodies served with soups and sandwiches and coffees. These days all the baking is done at the 11 Street store—the original Inglewood bakery was closed in 2001—and is sent out to the satellites to ensure quality and consistency within the group.

There's a healthy approach to much of the food (maybe it's something to do with those hospital outlets), and the tone sits well with those who want to linger over a book or a magazine. Wherever they are, the Good Earth cafes have become popular neighborhood gathering places and quiet refuges from the bustle around them.

Grand Isle

128 – 2 Avenue SE

Chinese (Cantonese)

TELEPHONE
269-7783

HOURS
Monday – Friday
10 AM – 2:30 PM;
5 PM – 10 PM
Saturday & Sunday
9 AM – 3 PM;
5 PM – 11 PM

RESERVATIONS
Accepted

BEVERAGES
Fully licensed

CARDS
Visa, MasterCard, Debit

Nonsmoking
Takeout & delivery

When it comes to rooms with a view, few can beat Grand Isle. This second-floor Chinatown restaurant occupies a flat-iron–style building that fronts on the Bow River, offering a great view of the water and Centre Street Bridge. The south-facing side has a view of the streets of Chinatown, fairly interesting in itself.

Aside from the view, Grand Isle has a multitude of dining choices, from various menus to dim sum to a buffet. All provide good quality and a selection of some of the more contemporary Cantonese food in the city.

Dim sum is a relaxing way to lunch—the heightened expectation that accompanies each cart as it pulls up to your table enhances the taste of the food. And with some thought, dim sum can be done in under $10 per person. However, it seems I'm always in a hurry here, so I usually head to the $7.50 lunch buffet for a good go-through of noodles, ginger beef, dumplings and a couple of soups. I've never been disappointed.

Indulge

620 – 8 Avenue SW

Casual Gourmet

TELEPHONE
229-9029

HOURS
Monday – Friday
7 AM – 4 PM
Sunday
9 AM – 2:30 PM
(not open Saturday)

RESERVATIONS
Accepted (recommend-
ed for weekend brunch)

BEVERAGES
Nonalcoholic only

CARDS
Visa, American Express,
Diners Club, Debit

Nonsmoking
Takeout, delivery &
catering

Aside from the hotels and coffee bars, there are surprisingly few decent sit-down places for breakfast in downtown. The folks who set up Indulge in 2000 saw this gap and created a serious market for their roasted pepper and brie omelets, their French toast with candied almonds and maple syrup, and their bottom-less cups of coffee.

Great to have this breakfast option. The owners have to open early anyway to work on all the catering orders they have for office lunches. That's Indulge's major trade but the space they use beside the Uptown Theatre is large enough to hold about sixty customers, so they included a cafe as well. The room is also a calm escape from the hustle and bustle of the city.

Every day, office workers line up to order breakfast and lunch from the overhead chalk-board. The menu changes daily, but it always includes a couple of soups, some robust sand-wiches and fresh baking. Good stuff; it's possi-ble to indulge heartily without breaking the bank.

Jonas'

937 – 6 Avenue SW

Hungarian

TELEPHONE
262-3302

HOURS
Monday – Wednesday
11:30 AM – 2 PM;
5 PM – 8 PM
Thursday – Friday
11:30 AM – 2 PM;
5 PM – 9 PM
Saturday
5 PM – 10 PM

RESERVATIONS
Recommended

BEVERAGES
Fully licensed

CARDS
Visa, MasterCard,
American Express, Debit

Nonsmoking
Takeout

We don't see a lot of Hungarian food these days. Eastern European foods generally are considered fairly high-fat and high-starch, so they have become culinary outcasts of late. However, Hungarian is perhaps the most elegant of these cuisines and is represented well at Jonas'.

Named after its owners—Janos and Rozsa Jonas—the restaurant is a long, narrow cinderblock room that is hidden in the shadows of a big apartment building. It's decorated with Hungarian weavings and photos, and is pleasantly homey and unassuming.

The menu rolls out the Hungarian faves, from chicken paprikash and bean goulash to beef stew with egg drop noodles and crepes stuffed with ground nuts and chocolate sauce. It's tasty, robust fare with a small order of paprikash filling Catherine for $4.65 and the goulash a warming bowl for $2.75 or $4.95. With a variety of fresh salads and a plate of cabbage rolls, the menu also offers a good vegetarian option. And you can't go wrong with a big glass of Hungarian wine for $3.

Juiced

2015 – 4 Street SW

263, 1632 – 14 Street NW (North Hill Shopping
Centre)

2000 Airport Road NE (Calgary International
Airport)

317, Banff Avenue, Banff (Cascade Plaza)

Juice Bar

TELEPHONE
4 Street
209-6552
North Hill Shopping
Centre
220-1846
Calgary International
Airport
503-8925
Cascade Plaza
760-3889

HOURS
Monday – Friday
8 AM – 7 PM
Saturday & Sunday
9 AM – 7 PM
(Hours may vary at
individual locations)

RESERVATIONS
Not accepted

BEVERAGES
Nonalcoholic only

CARDS
Visa, Debit

Nonsmoking
Takeout
Outdoor benches at 4
Street location

Aside from a few of the more vegetarian
entries in this book, Juiced is probably the
healthiest place for miles around. It is a fully
liquefied operation that has popped up with a
variety of smoothies, fresh juices and boosts.
You can get a Peach Passion smoothie with
peaches, bananas and peach sorbet. Or a
Cranberry Crush with cranberry juice, straw-
berries and raspberry sorbet. Poured into large,
low environmental impact Styrofoam cups
(their use is justified on lengthy posters), these
smoothies are very good.

I also like the fresh juices, twelve-ounce
squeezes of combos such as tomato, carrot,
beet, pepper, parsley and celery or carrot,
apple, beet and ginger. They also squeeze a lot
of wheat grass juice. Served in shot glasses or
espresso cups, wheat grass is the beverage of
choice for many healthy types.

Juiced also offers a brief list of sandwiches
(in the Calgary locations only), including roast
turkey, honey-cured ham and vegetarian. They
are far tastier than I might expect in such a
healthy place.

Kaffa

2138 – 33 Avenue SW

*Eclectic
Southwestern*

TELEPHONE
240-9133

HOURS
Monday – Friday
7 AM – midnight
Saturday
8 AM – midnight
Sunday
9 AM – 10 PM

RESERVATIONS
Not accepted

BEVERAGES
Fully licensed

CARDS
Cash only

Smoking Tuesdays,
Thursdays & Saturdays
7 AM – 6 PM in front
section only
Takeout
Patio

A little brown house known as Kaffa sits on 33 Avenue as one of the anchors of Marda Loop. Over the years it has become a community gathering place for many Loopers and others from around town who just like the atmosphere.

Kaffa has the tone of a '70s granola bar with much better food. It is a coffee house with a long list of accompanying banana breads, Rice Krispie squares and big chocolate chip cookies. In other words: munchie heaven.

But they also do a Southwestern menu of bean burritos, tamales and taco salads — nothing too elaborate but in keeping with the tone of the place. There is also a more eclectic list of shepherd's pie, bagels and brioche. And the soup and salad special comes in at $6.45.

Kaffa is laid back, friendly and a bit of a flashback. If you look closely, you will see granola on the menu too.

Kane's Harley Diner

1209 – 9 Avenue SE

Diner

TELEPHONE
269-7311

HOURS
Sunday – Thursday
7 AM – 9 PM
Friday & Saturday
7 AM – 10 PM

RESERVATIONS
Accepted

BEVERAGES
Fully licensed

CARDS
Visa, MasterCard,
American Express,
Diners Club, Debit

Nonsmoking section
Takeout
Patio

If you like the idea of chomping down your burger or bacon and eggs while basking in an orange glow, surrounded by Harley-Davidson bikes and memorabilia, Kane's Harley Diner may be the place for you. This is not one of those pseudo-reality theme restaurants either— this is the real deal. The diner used to be the showroom and repair shop for Kane's Harley dealership, which moved across the alley when the old liquor store became available. (That burned down a few years ago, but they have since rebuilt.)

The menu is the substantial grub that keeps bikers in fighting trim—flathead pancakes, liver and onions, chili, meat loaf, pork chops and big milk shakes. There's even a salad on the menu, although I've never seen anyone eating one.

Kane's is also a friendly place, where denizens of the Inglewood area antique shops and Loose Moose Theatre mingle with leather-clad bikers. These days a lot of those bikers are mom-and-pop groups visiting Kane's as part of a Harley pilgrimage.

Karma

2139 – 33 Avenue SW

Local Arts House

TELEPHONE
217-7955

HOURS
Monday – Thursday
11 AM – midnight
Friday
11 AM – 1 AM
Saturday
10 AM – 1 AM
Sunday
10 AM – midnight

RESERVATIONS
Not accepted
(Tickets presold for
some events)

BEVERAGES
Fully licensed

CARDS
Visa, MasterCard,
American Express, Debit

Smoking except non-
smoking for Saturday &
Sunday brunch
Takeout
Covered patio

At first glance Karma looks and smells like the dark, smoky, funky hangout it is. The scent of tobacco and beer fills the air even at a sunny lunch, and a bar and a stage dominate the room. But Karma is much more than that; it is a "Local Arts House" that offers a decent menu and live acoustic entertainment every evening.

Karma occupies a prominent street corner in Marda Loop and regularly packs the place for the likes of Tom Phillips and the Men of Constant Sorrow, Jenny Allen, Andrea Revel and Tim Williams. The feeling is intimate, and the music is a steal with usually small cover charges. Within the haze of smoke, customers often have something to eat. There are some tasty soup and sandwich specials such as ginger-carrot peppercorn shrimp for $8, and salads and wraps hovering around the $10 mark. Plus, there are some over-the-top cheesecakes and something called a Cherry Bang Belly Brownie. Rock on!

Lazy Loaf & Kettle

8 Parkdale Crescent NW

130 – 9 Avenue SE (Glenbow Museum)

Bakery Cafe

TELEPHONE
Parkdale Crescent
270-7810
Glenbow Museum
266-1002

HOURS
Parkdale Crescent NW
Monday – Friday
7 AM – 11 PM
Saturday & Sunday
8 AM – 10 PM
Glenbow Museum
Monday – Friday
7:30 AM – 4 PM
Saturday & Sunday
11 AM – 4 PM

RESERVATIONS
Not accepted

BEVERAGES
Beer & wine only

CARDS
Visa, MasterCard,
American Express, Debit

Nonsmoking
Takeout & catering
Patio at Parkdale
Cresent location

The two Lazy Loafs (Loaves?) produce a line of baking and sandwiches of immense proportions and significant quality. The most damning thing I can say about them is that some people find them just too big to get their mouths around.

The sandwiches are made from thick slices of their Kettle Bread—a nine-grain loaf that contains carrots, wheat germ and barley malt but no dairy, eggs or fat. (It's great for toast too.) Served with a bowl of house-made soup, the pair make a substantial lunch. Many folks order the half-sandwich and soup partly because of the size and partly to save room for dessert. Also served in mega sizes, the Nanaimo bars and puffed wheat squares and cookies are a down-home treat. Usually, one is enough for two customers unless you have a serious sweet tooth.

The downtown location in the Glenbow Museum offers a great break for both museum visitors and convention attendees, with some of the better coffee in the area.

Leo Fu's

511 – 70 Avenue SW

Chinese (Szechwan & Mandarin)

TELEPHONE
255-2528

HOURS
Monday – Friday
11:30 AM – 2 PM
Sunday – Thursday
4:30 PM – 10 PM
Friday & Saturday
4:30 PM – 11:30 PM

RESERVATIONS
Recommended

BEVERAGES
Fully licensed

CARDS
Visa, MasterCard,
American Express,
Diners Club

Nonsmoking section
Takeout

Leo Fu's menu contains some of the best and tastiest Chinese cuisine in the city—General Tso's chicken, orange beef, salt and pepper squid, Szechwan chicken wings. Chicken wings? Only the best wings I've ever had, dripping in chili-infused oil. (Don't think there's anything remotely healthy about them; they're just great.)

In truth, most of Leo Fu's menu pushes beyond the financial range of this book. (10 wings are $8.) But the weekday buffet is a bargain-packed $7.50, one of the best deals you'll find anywhere near Macleod Trail. And it's good quality stuff too—grilled dumplings, often their own ginger beef (not as sweet and sticky as many), always crisp vegetables and some kind of noodle. I always say that one pass through the buffet will suffice but always find myself up for a second visit.

The room is a rich blue and gold, the staff are pleasantly efficient and the food is unbeatable. Leo Fu's is still the best.

Lion's Den

234 – 17 Avenue SE

Diner

TELEPHONE
265-8482

HOURS
Daily 9 AM – 10 PM

RESERVATIONS
Accepted

BEVERAGES
Fully licensed

CARDS
Visa, MasterCard,
American Express

No nonsmoking section
Takeout

Given the glut of retro-diners that have appeared on the market recently, it's easy to overlook a place that has been a diner for ages—the Lion's Den. Sitting quietly at the intersection of 17 Avenue and Macleod Trail SE just outside the Stampede Grounds, the Den is a popular pre-Flames meeting place and one of the better cafes to eat in while attending the Stampede itself.

The Lion's Den is rich with Olympic, Stampede, Stampeder and Flames memorabilia. It's the kind of place where practically anyone who is anyone has eaten and likely enjoyed a clubhouse sandwich ($6) or fish & chips ($6.50) or even the veal cutlets ($6.50). Now where else can you even find a veal cutlet these days?

The food is all cooked and served by Rose and Rico Festa, two of the liveliest and most personable restaurateurs in the business. Rico will regale you with bizarre jokes while Rose cooks up a storm. And the Lion's Den is worth the visit just to recall how real Naugahyde feels.

Little Chef

555 Strathcona Boulevard SW (Strathcona
   Shopping Centre)

Family Dining

TELEPHONE
242-7219

HOURS
Monday – Saturday
11 AM – 8:30 PM
Saturday
9 AM – 9 PM
Sunday
9 AM – 8 PM

RESERVATIONS
Recommended

BEVERAGES
Fully licensed

CARDS
Visa, MasterCard, Debit

Nonsmoking
Takeout & catering
Patio

In the realm of high-quality family dining, few places are better than Little Chef. Owned and operated by Arthur Raynor, a former president of the Canadian Academy of Chefs, Little Chef provides variety, value and an impressively high quality of food.

Oh, it's not fancy-schmancy—it's still family dining after all. But you'll be hard-pressed to find a better steak and kidney pie in the city—lots of meat, flaky pastry, thick gravy—and for $9 with fries or a salad a very good deal. (Take-home frozen for $5!) And we're talking decent salad here too. Pick from spinach or tossed green or caesar—all with dressings that amplify the quality of the food.

Want a good burger, a beef dip, Belgian waffles or fish and chips? It's all here plus the ever-popular liver and onions on special evenings. (Book ahead for that—it really is popular.)

You can't beat the parking either, and on a warm evening, the patio is just dandy.

Malacca Moose

502 – 25 Avenue SW

International

TELEPHONE
282-0988

HOURS
Daily 8 AM – 7:30 PM
(Extended hours mid-
June to mid-September)

RESERVATIONS
Accepted

BEVERAGES
Nonalcoholic only

CARDS
MasterCard, American
Express, Debit

Nonsmoking
Takeout
Patio

True to its name, Malacca Moose is a multi-cultural blend of Malaysian and Canadian with a fair dose of French thrown in. The menu crosses borders with a chicken satay sandwich, ham and asparagus crepes, and scrambled eggs and toast, not to mention bouchee a la Reine, bacon and leek soup, and salami and Swiss cheese sandwiches.

The setting is just about as wacky, with a few tables wrapped around the kitchen and international knick-knacks on the walls. It's part tiki room and part bistro. A protected patio provides a pleasant seating area looking onto a small stretch of 4 Street NW.

Malacca Moose also houses the northern outpost of the Eiffel Tower bakery. Not exactly discount goods, just simply some of the best breads and pastries on the market. Many of them are used on the menu in dishes that rarely top $5. The flavors here are good. The service can be a bit slow, but the quality for the price is outstanding.

Marathon

130 – 10 Street NW

924 – 17 Avenue SW

Ethiopian

TELEPHONE
10 Street
283-6796
17 Avenue
802-1588

HOURS
Monday – Friday
11 AM – 2:30 PM,
5 PM – 10 PM
Saturday
11 AM – 11 PM
Sunday
5 PM – 10 PM

RESERVATIONS
Recommended

BEVERAGES
Fully licensed

CARDS
Visa, MasterCard,
American Express,
Diners Club, Debit

Nonsmoking
Takeout, delivery &
catering
Patio at 17 Avenue
location

The Ethiopian calendar designates about two hundred days each year as vegetarian. With such a strong commitment to a nonmeat diet, the culture has developed a long list of rich, flavorful and interesting foods. There are more creative lentil, cabbage and bean dishes (no nuts!) than you'll find in most vegetarian restaurants. And the flavors—mustards, berbere (a blend of chilies) and niter kibeh (butter with herbs) are outstanding.

For the carnivores there are tons of options too, from the yebeg wat (braised lamb in berbere) and the doro wat (chicken in lemon, garlic, ginger and berbere) to the kitfo (beef with hot peppers and niter kibeh).

The food is presented without utensils, to be scooped up with injera, the traditional bread made with the millet flour called teff. (For those uneasy about eating by hand, there are a few forks kicking around.) Most dishes are under $10, with major combos around $12 per person. The big bargain is a lunch buffet at both locations for $8.

The Mecca

10231 West Valley Road SW

Diner & Southern Barbecue

TELEPHONE
288-2500

WEB SITE
www.meccacafe.ca

HOURS
Monday – Sunday
7 AM – 3 PM
Friday – Sunday
5 PM – last guest

RESERVATIONS
Not accepted

BEVERAGES
Fully licensed

CARDS
Visa, MasterCard,
American Express, Debit

Nonsmoking section
Takeout
Patio

The Mecca is the closest thing we have in Calgary to a real roadhouse diner. A couple of decades ago, a trailer was plunked onto a gravel lot on the west end of town near what is now the Stoney Trail intersection with the Trans-Canada. Over time, extra rooms were added, but the look hasn't changed much.

The Mecca has always been known for abundant, high-quality breakfasts served to the skiing crowd that meets here before heading to the mountains. But recently the Mecca has added a line of weekend barbecue dishes and live entertainment to give it even more of a roadhouse feel. It is very good barbecue—it serves a variety of beef brisket and ribs, pork butt and ribs, and chicken that have all been slow-smoked in the Southern U.S. barbecue tradition. For $15, you get a choice of meats, plus baked beans, coleslaw, corn bread and a bun. The atmosphere is perfect for this kind of full-tilt, messy food. Don't wear anything too fancy.

Mekong

2885 – 17 Avenue SE

Vietnamese

TELEPHONE
248-1488

HOURS
Tuesday – Sunday
10 AM – 9 PM
Monday
10 AM – 4 PM

RESERVATIONS
Accepted

BEVERAGES
Fully licensed

CARDS
Visa, MasterCard, Debit

Nonsmoking section
Takeout & delivery
Patio (pending at press
time)

There are a lot of run-of-the-mill Vietnamese noodle shops out there. But one that distinguishes itself as a cut above many is the Mekong, which perches on 17 Avenue SE just east of Deerfoot Trail. It's a tiny, not terribly pretty place that serves a delicate, well-balanced version of a cuisine that is so often mishandled.

The difference is seen in the lightness of the cha gio filling and in the abundance of greens served with it. The oils are lower across the menu and attention is paid to the flavors and the freshness of the food. The salad rolls are an elegant blend of noodles and shrimp and some nicely sliced pork.

The caramel shrimp comes as a huge pile of beautifully flavored shrimp for a startling $9.75 and the lemongrass chicken features three large breasts for $8.25. Even the rice is particularly tasty. You can eat very well here for very cheap while sharing with a group or by indulging in the big bowls of bun—all under $10.

Midori

1054 – 17 Avenue SW

Japanese

TELEPHONE
244-3787

HOURS
Monday – Friday
11 AM – 10 PM
Saturday
Noon – 10 PM

RESERVATIONS
Not accepted

BEVERAGES
Fully licensed

CARDS
Visa, MasterCard,
American Express, Debit

No nonsmoking section
Takeout
Patio

Midori is a simple, sunny room facing 17 Avenue and packed with five tables, a five-seat counter and a menu that covers sushi, noodles and a small range of other dishes. Everything is crammed into the one room, with takeout containers stored in overhead bins and the full cooking process on view.

One combination meal offers chicken teriyaki and sushi with soup, rice and salad for $9.95. The Midori house special, a selection of sushi, yakitori, miso soup, salad and white string pickles is an equally reasonable $9.95. Served on a cafeteria tray, the miso soup swims with chunks of tofu and ribbons of nori. The salad is iceberg lettuce with a French-style dressing—nothing fancy but crisp and light. The highlight is the yakitori: three skewers of chicken breast with a slice of grilled green onion between each poultry piece. And the sushi is not bad, but they don't use raw fish— it's all cooked or smoked, which is just fine considering the surroundings.

Montreal Bagels

8408 Elbow Drive SW

Bagels

TELEPHONE
212-4060

HOURS
Monday – Saturday
8 AM – 6 PM
Sunday
9 AM – 6 PM

RESERVATIONS
Not accepted

BEVERAGES
Fully licensed

CARDS
Cash or cheque only

Nonsmoking
Takeout

The simply named Montreal Bagels has recently opened on the southeast corner of the intersection of Elbow and Heritage Drives. Owned by Ramesh Sivadnanam, a former baker at Montreal's St-Viateur Bakery, Montreal Bagels does the hand-rolled, boiled in honeyed water and baked in a wood-fired oven style of bagels. St-Viateur, operating since 1957, has a couple of outlets in Montreal and is generally considered to be one of the better and more traditional bagel bakeries in the city.

Montreal Bagels makes the basics—plain, poppyseed, sesame and multigrain bagels—and can put together some simple sandwiches. But the shop has room for tables, so the plan is to expand it into a cafe with a range of smoked meat and salmon bagels. Montreal Bagels sell their products for a competitive 55¢ each or $6 for a dozen and my ex-Montreal bagel fans tell me they are just like the ones from back home.

Mudder's & Faudder's

5421 – 11 Street NE

Newfoundland

TELEPHONE
275-2900

HOURS
Monday – Saturday
11 AM – 10 PM
Sunday
12 PM – 8 PM

RESERVATIONS
Not accepted

BEVERAGES
Fully licensed

CARDS
Visa, MasterCard,
American Express, Debit

Nonsmoking section
Takeout & delivery

Given the number of Newfoundlanders who have to come to Calgary over the years, it was just a matter of time before a Newfoundland restaurant opened to feed the passion for fish and chips with dressing and the propensity to serve hamburger meat as a side dish. Mudders was so successful in its original location on 17 Avenue SE that it had to move to larger digs in the northeast.

It's now Mudder's & Faudder's but is still packed with east coast hospitality, big platters of seafood and chips or liver and onions, and more than a little tobacco smoke. The big meal on the menu is a chunk of cod, four shrimp, four scallops, clam strips, a healthy dollop of coleslaw and a whole hill of fries for $15. That's a lot of eatin', b'y.

Mudder's & Faudder's also acts as one of the key gathering places for all the folks from The Rock. It's a guaranteed good time—don't go expecting a quiet evening. It's fun, loud and high fat, just like back home.

Nellie's

2308 – 4 Street SW (4 Street)

738 – 17 Avenue SW (The Original)

516 – 9 Avenue SW (Nellie's Breaks the Fast)

1001 – 17 Avenue SW (Cosmic Cafe)

1414 Kensington Road NW (Kensington)

Breakfast Cafe

TELEPHONE
4 Street
209-2708
The Original
244-4616
Nellie's Breaks the Fast
265-5071
Cosmic Cafe
806-2377
Kensington
283-0771

HOURS
Monday – Friday
7:30 AM – 3:30 PM
Saturday & Sunday
8:30 AM – 3:30 PM
(later at Cosmic Cafe)

RESERVATIONS
Accepted (sometimes)

BEVERAGES
Beer & wine at Cosmic
Cafe & Break the Fast

CARDS
Visa, MasterCard, Debit

Nonsmoking
Takeout
Patios at all but 4 Street
location

Nellie's used to be a tiny, single location on 17 Avenue SW serving a big breakfast to a long line of hungry Calgarians who clogged the sidewalk. Simple concept, big crowd. So the Nellie's empire expanded to five locations, including a second one on 17 Avenue. They are fairly small, serve basically the same menu in the same atmosphere, and now, instead of one lineup, there are five. Of course there are those who declare the food at one to be better than another, but regardless, they are all busy.

Nellie's calling card is the Belly Buster, which, at $8.75, includes three eggs, a choice of bacon, ham or sausage, a choice of french toast or pancakes, toast and hash browns. The rest of your culinary day is likely to be light unless plowing a field is on your agenda. Nellie's also does soup and sandwich lunches, and typically has a friendly, if off-kilter and funky, service style.

Opa!

1512 – 14 Street SW

6455 Macleod Trail South (Chinook Centre)

3625 Shaganappi Trail NW (Market Mall)

100 Anderson Road SE (South Centre)

324, 8 Avenue SW (TD Square)

Greek Fast Food

TELEPHONE
14 Street
245-5912
Chinook Centre
253-3323
Market Mall
247-0777
South Centre
271-7771
TD Square
262-4849

HOURS
Monday – Saturday
11 AM – 9 PM
(Mall outlet hours may
vary)

RESERVATIONS
Not accepted

BEVERAGES
Nonalcoholic only

CARDS
Cash only

Nonsmoking
Takeout

If the big blue banner with white *Opa!* lettering isn't a dead giveaway that this is a Greek place, the waft of garlic when you open the door is. Opa! is a Greek fast food operation that has four mall outlets and one free-standing cafe.

The cafe is bathed in the glare of fluorescents, washed by a hyperactive ventilation system and pounded by head-banging hits. It seems built to move you out quickly. But then again, it is not lingering food.

Opa! makes ordering simple by mounting colorful, numbered photos of the souvlaki and salads on the wall. So you can choose by name or number, or by just pointing at the picture. Once delivered on toss-away plates, the food is not bad. It's not great either—this is unbalanced, industrial fare—but it is mostly hot, fresh and, if you like Greek sauces, absolutely inundated in them. And frankly, I've had worse calamari in much tonier places.

Oriental Dallas

3855 – 17 Avenue SW

Vietnamese

TELEPHONE
217-8888

HOURS
Monday – Thursday
11 AM – 10 PM
Friday & Saturday
11 AM – 11 PM
Sunday
11:30 AM – 9 PM

RESERVATIONS
Accepted

BEVERAGES
Fully licensed

CARDS
Visa, MasterCard, Diners
Club, Debit

Nonsmoking
Takeout & delivery

The concentration of good Vietnamese noodle shops seems to be largely in and around the downtown core and out on 17 Avenue SE. That's so common that when I was told about Oriental Dallas on 17th, I went out to Forest Lawn looking for it—and found a Taco Bell instead.

So I took the quick trip west to Glendale to find Oriental Dallas tucked into a strip mall. It's a nice little place—all cozy booths providing a good level of privacy. It's clean and fresh, and the staff hustle about briskly.

The menu includes the current Vietnamese noodle faves plus some Thai, Cantonese and Beijing dishes. We tried both the salad rolls and the Vietnamese spring rolls and were impressed by the salad rolls and depressed by the oiliness of the spring rolls. Edible but not great. The bun was about the same—it's okay but not the lightest or best balanced we've had. Still, for the price and the location, Oriental Dallas is worth a quick lunch if you're in the area.

Pelican Pier

4404 – 14 Street NW

Family Seafood Restaurant

TELEPHONE
289-6100

HOURS
Monday – Thursday
11 AM – 9 PM
Friday & Saturday
11 AM – 10 PM
Sunday
12 PM – 9 PM

RESERVATIONS
Not accepted

BEVERAGES
Fully licensed

CARDS
Visa, MasterCard, Debit

Nonsmoking 5 PM – 8
PM, nonsmoking section
otherwise
Takeout & delivery

While judging an oyster-shucking competition with some seafood professionals, I asked where they would go for some good fish and chips. One responded with the name Pelican Pier on the northern shores of 14 Street across from the Winter Club.

So I went.

And I was impressed with the overall quality of the food, the lightness of the batter on the fish, the richness of the chowder and the generally reasonable prices. This is all backed up by the fishy knowledge of the owner and his commitment to providing a pleasant, professional dining experience to his customers in a comfortable setting. It's that commitment that sees frequent lineups at his doors and a long list of return customers from across the city.

When in doubt, the two-piece pollock and chips dinner at $7.25 is a good bet. With house-made tartar sauce, a good cole slaw and fresh-cut chips, it's a hearty meal.

Peppino

1240 Kensington Road NW

Italian Deli

TELEPHONE
283-5350

HOURS
Monday – Friday
10 AM – 6 PM
Saturday
10 AM – 5 PM

RESERVATIONS
Not accepted

BEVERAGES
Nonalcoholic only

CARDS
Visa, MasterCard

Nonsmoking
Takeout & catering
Patio

There are only four tables and about a dozen stools in Peppino, but in spite of its physical limitations it packs a ton of Italian flavors and atmosphere. There's a big cooler with cold cuts and cheeses, another with drinks and gelati, and racks of risotto and pasta. And behind all the food, there's an Italian family who remember how it used to taste back home.

Ask for a sandwich, and they'll slice a mile-high pile of meats onto a crusty roll with cheeses and a spicy spread. And charge a bargain $6 for it. Ask for an ice cream cone, and you'll have to choose from among the dozen homemade gelati on sale that day. (Here's a hint: The Italian Kiss of chocolate and hazelnut is the current top seller with lemon being the number one sorbetto.) And they will charge you $2 for that.

You'll leave satisfied and longing for another appetite to bring you back for the friendly atmosphere. And for that they won't charge you at all.

Peter's Drive In

219 – 16 Avenue NE

Hamburgers

TELEPHONE
277-2747

HOURS
Daily 9 AM – midnight

RESERVATIONS
Not accepted

BEVERAGES
Nonalcoholic only

CARDS
Cash only

Nonsmoking
Takeout
Outdoor tables

As much a Calgary icon as the Husky—oops!—Calgary Tower, Peter's just keeps on putting out those burgers and fries. For many visitors a trip to Calgary is not complete without a double cheeseburger for $3.40 from this Trans-Canada drive-through.

Many locals agree, avoiding the Golden Arches to cue up at Peter's. Over the years the establishment has expanded to meet demand with a much larger parking lot and grassy dining area than there used to be. The owners even paid for a longer turn-in lane to be built off 16 Avenue.

All day, every day, snow or shine, there's a lineup as folks wait briefly for their cheeseburger/fries/shake meal for $7.40. But considering the volume, the crowd is surprisingly well behaved and tidy. And on sunny days all the tables (at least twenty-five) are packed with families and work groups. Note: there's no indoor seating here, so prepare your in-car cafe accordingly.

Pfanntastic Pannenkoek Haus

2439 – 54 Avenue SW

Dutch Pancakes

TELEPHONE
243-7757

HOURS
Tuesday – Friday
11 AM – 8 PM
Saturday & Sunday
8 AM – 8 PM

RESERVATIONS
Recommended Tuesday
– Saturday, not accepted
Sunday

BEVERAGES
Fully licensed

CARDS
Visa, MasterCard,
American Express, Debit

Nonsmoking

In a town that's famous for it's big, fluffy, Western-style pancakes, the appearance of a Dutch pancake house is of some note. We are familiar with the concept of pancakes in these parts, but these thinner, variably topped pancakes are unique.

Following the Dutch tradition, the Pfanntastic loads ham and mushrooms, bacon and leeks, apple sauce, warm cherries, or blueberries and ice cream onto the thin, almost crepey pannenkoeks. There's a bottle of stroop on each table for those who enjoy extra syrupy sweetness. And for the fully sweetened, there's a pancake of ice cream, whipped cream, kirsch in a chocolate cup, chocolate sauce and cherries. Whoa! It's also the most expensive pancake at $11. Most are $7 – $9.

The Pfanntastic is hidden in a strip mall near the intersection of Crowchild and Glenmore, but fans find it easily. Best to call ahead or arrive early. Expect to leave feeling much fuller than when you arrived but not much lighter in the wallet.

Pies Plus

12445 Lake Fraser Drive SE (Avenida Place)
Bragg Creek Shopping Centre, Bragg Creek

Pies & Light Meals

TELEPHONE
Avenida Place
271-6616
Bragg Creek Shopping
Centre
949-3450

HOURS
Avenida Place
Tuesday – Friday
8 AM – 9 PM
Saturday & Sunday
8 AM – 6 PM
Bragg Creek Shopping
Centre
Monday – Thursday
10 AM – 5 PM
Friday
10 AM – 6 PM
Saturday & Sunday
10 AM – 7 PM

RESERVATIONS
Not accepted

BEVERAGES
Nonalcoholic only

CARDS
Cash or cheque only at
Avenida Place location
Visa at Bragg Creek
Shopping Centre

Nonsmoking
Takeout
Patio at Avenida Place
location

The two Pies Plus locations have gained a solid reputation for high quality pie served in huge slabs or to take home. One hunk of their pie served with a big whap of ice cream could be considered a meal in itself, but in order to present a more balanced diet, I feel obliged to mention that there are other items on the menu at Pies Plus.

There are soups and sandwiches as well as muffins and quiche, and at any given lunchtime, you will find many folks happily enjoying them. It is easy to surmise that the only reason is so that they can justify a slice of apple or blueberry, but regardless, the lunches are hearty and well prepared. There's nothing complex about them, but the dishes fit the rustic, wholesome look of the place.

Pies Plus also makes a good cup of coffee and is a great pit stop if you're in the Bragg Creek area.

Pita's Plus Donair

3132 – 26 Street NE (Interpacific Business Park)

Lebanese

TELEPHONE
735-1116

HOURS
Monday – Friday
9 AM – 9 PM
Saturday
9 AM – 7 PM

RESERVATIONS
Accepted

BEVERAGES
Nonalcoholic only

CARDS
Cash only

Nonsmoking
Takeout

If you're really hungry, you may be able to spend $10 at Pita's Plus. That's if you have the chicken donair plus for $6 (that's the big one with roasted chicken, tomatoes, lettuce, onions and sweet or tahini sauce in a pita), a serving of tabouleh for $2 and a rice pudding for $2. But that's a big meal.

If you are economizing, the regular falafel, similarly wrapped in pita, runs $3, and the stuffed grape leaves are $2. So is the plain pita pie. Add 50¢ for cheese. Remarkable prices with high quality. This small, family-run, northeast cafe is worth the experience not only for value but for the welcome of the owners.

As for the rice pudding, it's some of the best in the city, regardless of price. It's creamy with the fragrance of rose water and a light dusting of cinnamon. Sure, the utensils are plastic, but this food is very real.

The Planet

2212 – 4 Street SW

101 Bowridge Drive NW

150 – 9 Avenue SW (PanCanadian Plaza)

3605 Manchester Road SE

Coffee Roaster & Cafe

TELEPHONE
4 Street
541-0960
Bowridge Drive
288-2233
PanCanadian Plaza
290-2200
Manchester Road
243-9992

HOURS
Daily 7 AM – midnight
(May vary at separate locations)

RESERVATIONS
Not accepted

BEVERAGES
Nonalcoholic only

CARDS
Visa, MasterCard, Debit

Nonsmoking
Takeout
Outdoor benches at 4 Street location

It doesn't really matter how far away my wife, Catherine, might be at the time, if her car happens to point even slightly toward 4 Street, she'll say, "Well, since I'm headed in that direction anyway, I might as well pop into The Planet for a coffee." A double espresso with a shot of hot milk that is (no foam, no toppings, please). Pump one of those into her, and she's good for a half-day.

Now, I don't recommend making a complete diet of Planet coffee, so I might advise picking up one of their grilled sandwiches or perhaps some of the baked goodies. At press time the 4 Street location was under expansion and was about to go nonsmoking, making all of the satellites fresh-air havens. In addition, they were talking of doing a Euro-style petit dejeuner of rolls and cheeses that would match their coffee perfectly. Hopefully, by the time you read this, the new menu will be a reality.

But, regardless of food, the coffee's on.

Pongo

524 – 17 Avenue SW

Contemporary Noodle House

TELEPHONE
209-1073

HOURS
Tuesday – Thursday
11:30 AM – 11 PM
Friday & Saturday
11:30 AM – 4:00 AM
Sunday
11:30 AM – 10 PM

RESERVATIONS
Not accepted

BEVERAGES
Fully licensed

CARDS
Visa, MasterCard,
American Express, Debit

Nonsmoking section
Takeout
Patio

When Pongo opened in the late '90s, it was the most cutting edge restaurant of the moment. The idea was to gather noodle recipes from across Asia—Pad Thai from Thailand, Cantonese chow mein, Japanese steak and shitake udon—and put them all on one menu for under $10 in a sleek room filled with other trendy people. It worked very well for a while, with folks lining up to get in.

Pongo still looks good with its strong metallic and wood tone, small television screens embedded in a dividing wall showing Japanimation and a sought-after patio on warm evenings. It's not as crowded as it used to be, but the menu has broadened somewhat to include rice bowls with teriyaki salmon, coconut curry stew, salt and pepper squid, and sake steamed mussels.

Pongo may no longer be the flavor of the moment, but the fact that it is still around and thriving is testament to the execution of the product and the quality of the experience.

Primal Grounds

3003 – 37 Street SW

2000 – 69 Street SW (Westside Recreation Centre)

Organic Bakery Cafe

TELEPHONE
37 Street
240-4185
Westside Centre
663-0137

WEB SITE
www.primalgrounds.com

HOURS
37 Street
Monday – Friday
7 AM – 11 PM
Saturday
8 AM – 11 PM
Sunday
8 AM – 10 PM
Westside Centre
Monday – Friday
7 AM – 9 PM
Saturday & Sunday
9 AM – 6 PM

RESERVATIONS
Accepted

BEVERAGES
Nonalcoholic only

CARDS
Cash only

Nonsmoking except on
patio at 37 Street
Takeout, delivery &
catering at 37 Street
Patio at 37 Street
Takeout at Westside
Centre

Now these people know how to slice a dessert. The carrot cake—rich, thick and drippy with cream cheese icing—is roughly the size of a small brick. Enough to satisfy three people. And those sandwiches—the roast turkey and cranberry is a three-hander. There's no delicate way to eat it, and what is particularly nice is that the bulk comes from the greenery. It's a salad and a sandwich in one!

Primal's owner declares that she sells happiness first and food second—an interesting corporate strategy. And it seems to work. Primal is filled from sunrise to sunset, and there's often a lineup at the drive-through window—a legacy of the former burger stand within which it resides.

Primal also makes a decent coffee and rounds out the menu with wraps, soups, jambalaya, jerk chicken and naked turtles. (Go see for yourself.) And at the Westside location, they are making great pizzas, including gluten-free ones.

Punjab

3132 – 26 Street NE (Interpacific Business Park)

Pakistani

TELEPHONE
250-6878

HOURS
Daily 11 AM – 2:30 PM;
5 PM – 11 PM

RESERVATIONS
Accepted

BEVERAGES
Nonalcoholic only

CARDS
Cash only

Nonsmoking
Takeout & delivery

You may notice a familiar address at the head of this review. There are four restaurants from the Interpacific Business Park in this book, the newest of which is the Punjab, which is also the only Pakistani restaurant in Calgary.

I have had limited exposure to the Punjab, but what I've had so far I've liked. If you are looking for a quiet lunch in the area, this is your best bet; as the newest eatery, it is also the least populated.

But if you are looking for great variety, you will be limited here. Although the Punjab is open daily from lunch through dinner, the lunch buffet is all of two buffet trays long. So perhaps a half-dozen dishes are offered. They are good—the curried goat is excellent as are the daal and a potato–eggplant mix. But in a world of mega-huge buffets it seems a bit skimpy. It was enough, however, to make me want to return for the longer dinner menu and more of the robust style of Pakistani cuisine.

Puspa

1051 – 40 Avenue NW

Indian (Bengali)

TELEPHONE
282-6444

WEB SITE
www.cadvision.com/
dattaj/puspa

HOURS
Monday – Thursday
5 PM – 10 PM
Friday
5 PM – 10:30 PM
Saturday
12 PM – midnight

RESERVATIONS
Recommended

BEVERAGES
Fully licensed

CARDS
Visa, MasterCard,
American Express,
Diners Club, Debit

Nonsmoking
Takeout & delivery

Puspa is not only the sole Bengali-style Indian restaurant in Calgary, it is also one of the very few Indian restaurants of any kind found in the northern part of the city. Which means it can be very busy on weekend evenings for both dine-in and takeout.

The Bengali style brings a robust, hearty level of spice to the food; there may not be as much cream as Kashmiri or as much complexity as some Punjabi offerings, but it is still very tasty. The food is skillfully prepared and served by an accommodating staff.

The best deal at Puspa is lunch. They do a short list of curries—lamb, beef, chicken, vegetable—in meal form with soup, salad, rice, dessert and coffee for between $6 and $7.50. Outstanding value. The curries are rich and intense, and although the breads are extra, they are very good too. At dinner things can get pricier, but Puspa remains one of the better Indian restaurants for value.

Rajdoot

2424 – 4 Street SW

Indian (Mughlai & Northern)

TELEPHONE
245-0181

HOURS
Monday – Friday
11:30 AM – 2 PM
Sunday – Thursday
5 PM – 10 PM
Friday & Saturday
5 PM – 11 PM

RESERVATIONS
Recommended

BEVERAGES
Fully licensed

CARDS
Visa, MasterCard,
American Express,
Diners Club, Debit

Nonsmoking
Takeout & delivery
Patio

Over the years, Rajdoot has gained a reputation as one of the finest all-round Indian restaurants in Calgary. It has achieved this with a fine blend of top-notch food, professional service and an overall commitment to service.

The menu at Rajdoot is extensive — and expensive. But you can easily find bargains in the buffets. On weekdays during lunch, there is always an elaborate display of dishes for $10, and on Sunday and Monday evenings, there is a major spread for $15. The buffet is well tended, with small portions being put out regularly so nothing has a chance to depreciate, and the breads are always hot.

The biggest hit, though, is the Tuesday evening vegetarian buffet for $13. Very nice foods, rich curries, creamy daals, chickpeas in many forms — and very busy. (Catherine loves the potatoes and the paneer.) It's the kind of buffet where your carnivore friends can discovered that there is much more to food than meat.

Restaurant Indonesia

1604 – 14 Street SW

Indonesian

TELEPHONE
244-0645

HOURS
Tuesday – Friday
11:30 AM – 2:30 PM;
5 PM – 11 PM
Saturday
5 PM – 11 PM
Sunday
5 PM – 9 PM

RESERVATIONS
Recommended

BEVERAGES
Fully licensed

CARDS
Visa, MasterCard,
American Express

Nonsmoking
Takeout

One of the best all-round deals for good food, decent price, fine service and a nice setting is lunch at the Restaurant Indonesia. I'll even throw in moderately healthy, making this a must-visit place. Plus, it's great for vegetarians.

In the evening the restaurant presents the full-blown, elegant cuisine of Indonesia. Great satay, beautiful nasi goreng, a bizarrely savory soy dish called aduk aduk tempeh and much more. You could do the rijsttafel with a multitude of small dishes Dutch-style, but that will push the price over $20.

At lunch, however, you can indulge in curry beef, sweet and sour prawns, creamy basil chicken or pork in oyster sauce, each with rice and vegetables for under $7. They even have the popular satay with peanut sauce with rice and noodles for the same price.

The setting is very comfortable with the walls adorned in colorful carved Indonesian masks, and the service is as personable and professional as you can get. It is truly amazing that lunch here is so cheap.

Reto and the Machine

315 Stephen Avenue Walk SW (+30 level,
Bankers Hall)

*Quick Gourmet
Pasta*

TELEPHONE
261-5020

HOURS
Monday – Wednesday
10 AM – 6 PM
Thursday & Friday
10 AM – 8 PM
Saturday
10 AM – 5:30 PM

RESERVATIONS
Not accepted

BEVERAGES
Nonalcoholic only

CARDS
Visa, MasterCard, Debit

Nonsmoking
Takeout

A few years ago a Swiss chef named Reto
Mathis had a problem with his pasta. It would-
n't cook easily at his St. Moritz restaurant
because of the high altitude. Water would boil
at 87°C, not a high enough temperature for
good pasta cooking.

So Mathis developed a pressurized cooking
system that pushed the temperature to 130°C,
and he made a thin-walled pasta to cook in it.
The result was perfect pasta in a remarkable
two minutes.

That technology is being used at the new
Reto and the Machine outlets springing up in
Canada. The one in the new Bankers Hall
Food Gallery features fourteen sauces—also
Swiss made—to go along with the spaghetti
and penne. They are good, flavorful recipes
with no additives or preservatives, and they create not only a fast but a moderately healthy
and cheap meal. The pastas range from $5 –
$6, with sauces from Red Lampang Curry to
Champignons de Foret. None have meat products, and few use any seafood, so they make
good vegetarian options too.

Rockin' Robin's

7007 – 11 Street SE

2033 – 16 Avenue NW

Diner

TELEPHONE
11 Street
252-3067
16 Avenue
289-8922

HOURS
Monday – Friday
7 AM – 10 PM
Saturday
7 AM – 9 PM
Sunday
8 AM – 8 PM

RESERVATIONS
Accepted for groups of
8 or more

BEVERAGES
Beer & wine

CARDS
Visa, MasterCard,
American Express, Debit

Nonsmoking
Takeout

Rockin' Robin's is not quite a chain yet, but it could well be some day. The restaurants are a '50s offspring of the Humpty's family, and there are currently two outlets in Calgary and a third in Red Deer.

The look is full-on retro-diner with yards of red vinyl and nouveau arborite. It's not vintage, but it is a very good replication. There are booths, a long counter and a menu that can answer any '50s yearning.

Robin's offers hot turkey and hamburger sandwiches, meat loaf, pork chops, liver and onions, bacon and eggs, pancakes, and chili dogs. And it is plate-covering, belly-filling grub. Don't look for spices here, but if gravy is your desire, it shall be answered. Some of the big dinners creep over the $10 mark, but most items remain well under it.

Staff continue the diner theme with appropriate uniforms and attitude, creating an atmosphere that is comfortable for all ages. It's a fine place to take the kids or the grandparents for an ice cream float or a piece of banana cream pie.

Rocky's Burgers

4645 – 12 Street SE

Hamburgers

TELEPHONE
243-0405

HOURS
Winter
Monday – Friday
9 AM – 4 PM
Summer
Monday – Friday
9 AM – 4 PM
Saturdays
10 AM – 3 PM

RESERVATIONS
Not accepted

BEVERAGES
Nonalcoholic only

CARDS
Cash only

Nonsmoking
Takeout only
6 outdoor tables

The big red bus sits hip deep in prairie grasses surrounded by pickup trucks, minivans and expensive cars. A small crowd waits patiently near the side of the bus, where a small table of condiments leans gently into the gravel parking lot. An arm extends from the bus's window with a muffled voice behind it: "Cheeseburger with fries."

One of the milling crowd breaks forward and clutches the bag, opening it briefly to squeeze a long stream of ketchup into it. He heads to one of the six tables on the other side of the bus to scarf down his burger in the noon sun. His day is complete.

This is the scene at Rocky's Burgers every weekday throughout the year. And this busy day is in early January with a Chinook wind blowing.

Regardless of the weather, the lineup is long at Rocky's. Customers come for the huge, freshly prepared burgers, the hand-cut fries and the poutine. There's even a crowd that goes for the bacon and egg breakfast. Most expensive item? The double cheeseburger at $5.25.

Roti Hut

920 – 36 Street NE

Trinidad & Tobago

TELEPHONE
272-1672

HOURS
Monday – Saturday
11 AM – 9 PM
Sunday
10 AM – 8 PM

RESERVATIONS
Accepted

BEVERAGES
Fully licensed

CARDS
Visa, MasterCard, Debit

Nonsmoking
Takeout & catering

When it comes to fast and cheap, one of the tastiest—and often healthiest—meals is the Caribbean roti. That's where stewed meats and/or vegetables are rolled into a freshly baked roti bread. But finding some in Calgary is difficult, so it's great to find a place like the Roti Hut, which does its roti well.

The folks here use various fillings in their rotis from curried beef to jerk chicken to pure vegetables, with prices ranging from $4 – $11. They are both filling and tasty, with the curry chicken providing a tangy curry bite and a decent complement of potatoes. And they offer more than just rotis. There's also fried salt fish, doubles (chickpea sandwiches) and oxtail on the menu.

The Roti Hut also has the full range of Caribbean drinks and sweets to satisfy your Island hungers. And it's all served in a comfortably casual room with just a hint of the beaches.

Saigon

1221 – 12 Avenue SW

Vietnamese

TELEPHONE
228-4200

HOURS
Monday – Thursday
11 AM – 10 PM
Friday & Saturday
11 AM – 11 PM

RESERVATIONS
Recommended

BEVERAGES
Fully licensed

CARDS
Visa, MasterCard,
American Express,
Diners Club

Nonsmoking section
Takeout

Not everything on Saigon's menu is cheap. But then again, this is not a typical Vietnamese noodle shop. Saigon is simply the best pure Vietnamese restaurant in Calgary.

The expertise shows in the delicate preparation of the Imperial rolls (five for $3.75) and the salad rolls (two for $3.75). The ingredients are all high quality, and the sauces are among the most elegant anywhere. In its best form, Vietnamese cuisine is fresh and light and riddled with intricate flavors. These are evident in the wide variety of the popular bun noodle dishes ranging from $6.75 – $10.75 (that's the one with satay shrimp and chicken).

For a more elaborate meal, there is the Genghis Khan grill, where customers cook raw meats on a perforated, curved grill that resembles the Asian warrior's helmet. The meats are then rolled with greens and sauces in thin rice wraps. The total cost is $20.75—but that's for two people. Well worth it.

Saigon Broadway

326 – 14 Street NW

Vietnamese

TELEPHONE
270-8648

HOURS
Monday – Saturday
11 AM – 9:30 PM

RESERVATIONS
Accepted

BEVERAGES
Beer & wine

CARDS
MasterCard, Debit

Nonsmoking
Takeout
Patio

There seems to be a multitude of "Saigon" restaurants around town. I suppose that's a good way to indicate that the restaurant is Vietnamese, but it can confusing when telling friends to meet at the Saigon.

The Saigon Broadway (a reference to the Broadway musical *Miss Saigon*) is a bright, sparkling clean room that seats thirty-four in tight quarters. Customers are given colorful, laminated menus that list about sixty dishes. You write your choice on a separate paper menu and pass it to the server, who brings the food very quickly.

The fare is largely a variety of the currently popular soups and noodle dishes featuring freshly grilled shrimp, lemongrass chicken and salad rolls among other Vietnamese delights. It's fresh, lightly flavored, well served and cheap. It's almost impossible to eat more than $10 worth of food at Saigon Broadway. But it's fun trying.

Saigon Y2K

310 Centre Street S

Vietnamese

TELEPHONE
265-3035

HOURS
Sunday, Monday,
Wednesday & Thursday
11 AM – 8 PM
Tuesday
11 AM – 3 PM
Friday & Saturday
10 AM – 9 PM

RESERVATIONS
Recommended

BEVERAGES
Fully licensed

CARDS
Visa, MasterCard,
American Express,
Diners Club, Debit

Nonsmoking
Takeout, delivery &
catering

Remember Y2K? Seems so long ago. But it lives on in a little cafe fronting on Centre Street in the heart of Chinatown. Saigon Y2K is one of a number of Vietnamese restaurants to open in the area over the past few years that offer a range of light, fresh noodle and rice dishes.

Saigon Y2K distinguishes itself with its quality. The dishes seem particularly fresh, the greens a little crunchier, the sauces a little more sparkling than most of the rest. The salad rolls seem prepared to order, keeping all the ingredients from melding too much and preventing the rice wrappers from turning into stretchy tooth grabbers.

The bun is also light and fresh, with high quality nuoc mam (fish sauce), well-trimmed and grilled meats, a clear, tasty broth and nicely cooked noodles.

Service is quick and friendly, the decor is appropriately oddball (I love the backlit waterfall), and the food is cheap. I don't see anything on the menu over $9.

Sal's Deli

9140 Macleod Trail S (Newport Village)

Italian Deli

TELEPHONE
255-6011

HOURS
Monday – Friday
11:30 AM – 2:30 PM
Monday – Saturday
5 PM – 11 PM

RESERVATIONS
Not accepted

BEVERAGES
Nonalcoholic only

CARDS
Visa, MasterCard,
American Express, Debit

Nonsmoking
Takeout, delivery &
catering

Back before Da Salvatore's became a popular Italian restaurant in Acadia, there was Sal's Deli. It became so busy that owner Sal Monna and his family expanded into the restaurant. But that hasn't seemed to make the deli any less busy.

Sal's is a small but efficient one-stop Italian market. There are racks of risotto and pasta, cans of tuna and tomato sauce, and coolers filled with drinks, cold cuts, cheeses, marinated vegetables and seafood.

You can order some pasta dishes to eat at Sal's counter, but the best option is to ask for a freshly constructed sandwich. The staff will layer pretty much anything you want onto crusty Italian buns — the cold-cut sandwich might include prosciutto, Genoa salami and mortadella with some provolone or Friulano and some hot peppers. Or you can get a vegetarian with marinated eggplant, mushrooms and peppers. Great stuff, and a substantial lunch can be enjoyed for under $6. With a little espresso or a chinotto drink, it's a bella lunch break.

Skylark

5315 – 17 Avenue SE

Indian (Punjabi)

TELEPHONE
272-6313

HOURS
Tuesday – Friday
11 AM – 2 PM;
5 PM – 9 PM
Saturday
11 AM – 10 PM
Sunday
12 PM – 8 PM

RESERVATIONS
Accepted

BEVERAGES
Fully licensed

CARDS
Visa, MasterCard, Debit

Nonsmoking
Takeout & catering

The Skylark is the most eastern restaurant in this book—not because of its culture but because of its address. It's been just east of 52 Street SE on 17 Avenue for twelve years and just keeps on going strongly.

The Skylark has a clean, white dining room with a small bakery counter at the front filled with fresh burfi and jalebis and other sweets baked in-house. They serve a fairly typical menu of butter chicken, alu gobi and lamb korma for very good prices. Almost everything is under $10.

But what sets the Skylark aside is their lunches, a collection of thali combos. For $7 you can have two vegetable dishes and the three Rs of Indian cooking—rice, raita and roti. Go for meat instead of vegetables and the price goes up $2. Excellent value.

It's good food too, and it's served pleasantly in a relaxing atmosphere. Certainly worth the trip east.

Socrates' Corner

2640 Parkdale Boulevard NW

Bookstore Cafe

TELEPHONE
242-8042

HOURS
Monday – Wednesday
7 AM – 6 PM
Thursday & Friday
7 AM – 8 PM
Saturday
7 AM – 6 PM
Sunday
9 AM – 5 PM

RESERVATIONS
Not accepted

BEVERAGES
Nonalcoholic only

CARDS
Visa, MasterCard, Debit

Nonsmoking
Takeout

When Chapters and Indigo arrived a few years ago, they brought with them the idea of food and drink in bookstores. That broke through some old barriers and made a lot of people happy. It may have soiled a few books, but it also sold a lot more.

One of the independent booksellers who liked the idea was Linda O'Connor of Socrates' Corner. So when she moved her store from Strathcona to a sunny location on Parkdale Boulevard just west of Crowchild Trail, she incorporated a cafe. A nice one too, where you can grab an early coffee and muffin or an afternoon tea with scones or a decent soup and sandwich lunch. A good-sized roast turkey sandwich on multigrain bread with a hearty bowl of soup is $6.50 — very decent for the quality. And house-made muffins and scones are $1.35. Excellent value and you can catch up on your reading while you dine.

Sonoma Cafe

520 – 5 Avenue SW (+15 level, Northland Bank Tower)

California–Global

TELEPHONE
233-0111

HOURS
Monday – Friday
7 AM – 4 PM

RESERVATIONS
Not accepted

BEVERAGES
Fully licensed

CARDS
Visa, MasterCard,
American Express, Debit

Nonsmoking
Takeout, delivery &
catering
Indoor patio

Traipsing the Plus 15s can be depressing from a culinary perspective. Sure, it's great to avoid the chilly streets in January, but Food Fare fare can be pretty pedestrian (no pun intended). However, the Sonoma Cafe makes a distinct diversion from the ordinary. They actually cook things.

Things such as a Hungarian mushroom soup ($4.25 & $6.50), Spolumbo sausage and mushroom pizza ($11.50) and a grilled veggie sandwich ($8.25). The meat-loaf sandwich ($9) is a thick, hot, tasty sandwich slathered with honey Dijon mustard, and the peanut butter cookies ($2) are big enough to satisfy the whole office.

Service can be a bit frantic, but that is just the nature of the Plus 15 office tower beast. The room embraces the soft sandy tones of the southwest, but the tone carries the feel of the hurried rush of the office, with meetings spilling over into lunch. Every day the eighty seats are packed with more folks waiting for a seat. But they don't wait for long; it's back to work for most folks in under an hour.

Sorabol

628 – 8 Avenue SW

Korean

TELEPHONE
269-9858

HOURS
Monday – Friday
11:30 AM – 10 PM
Saturday & Sunday
12 PM – 10 PM

RESERVATIONS
Accepted

BEVERAGES
Fully licensed

CARDS
Visa, MasterCard,
American Express,
Diners Club, Debit

Nonsmoking section
Takeout & delivery

Korean food fans speak highly of Sorabol in the west end of downtown. I admit to having some difficulty with the cuisine myself—much of the spicing seems heavy-handed for my palate. But I like a table barbecue as well as the next person.

The Sorabol is a pleasant enough place, if a bit time locked. The room is large—it seats ninety—with very high ceilings and the pastels of the early '80s. It's divided almost totally into booths, providing a private dining experience. Most of the booths are outfitted with the table barbecues to cook bul-go-gi and be-bim-bap at your table.

Or you can just head to the $7 buffet for a quick scarf of Korean delights (some Chinese too). Every weekday lunch they trot out about twenty items from chili-packed chicken and ginger beef to fried dumplings and cold noodles—and kim chee, the distinctive chili-garlic-cabbage dish. Make sure you don't have any important meetings after lunch here.

Spolumbo's

1308 – 9 Avenue SE

Deli & Sausage Makers

TELEPHONE
264-6452

WEB SITE
www.spolumbos.com

HOURS
Monday – Saturday
8 AM – 5:30 PM

RESERVATIONS
Accepted for private
room only

BEVERAGES
Beer & wine only

CARDS
Visa, MasterCard, Debit

Nonsmoking
Takeout & catering

When the knees started to go, the Spoletini brothers and Mike Palumbo figured there had to be better things to do than beat up Eskimos on a frozen field in November. So they retired from their duties as Stampeders, brought team-mate Craig Watson along with them, borrowed some family recipes and opened Spolumbo's in Inglewood. In no time, their house-made spicy Italian sausage on a bun ($6) and drippy meat-loaf sandwich ($6.65) created a lineup that was out the door.

So they built a big new place with lots more room and a big plant to make even more kinds of sausage (chicken and apple, turkey and sundried tomato, etc.). And the lineup still reaches out the door. The quality is top notch, service is always good and the price is right. Watson has moved on to other projects, but the other guys are still there. And now they are selling sausages in the Eskimo end zone before the games—and doing a big touchdown dance on wonky knees.

Starlite

369 Heritage Drive SE

Neighborhood Cafe

TELEPHONE
255-3333

HOURS
Monday – Saturday
11 AM – 1 AM
Sunday
4 PM – 9 PM

RESERVATIONS
Accepted

BEVERAGES
Fully licensed

CARDS
Visa, MasterCard,
American Express, Debit

Nonsmoking section
Takeout & delivery

The Starlite is one of those classic cafes you'll find in most older neighborhoods and small towns. The menu covers everything from cannelloni to liver and onions, and fish and chips. There are VLTs in the lounge, and the overhead air cleaner does nothing to purify the heavy smoke. And it seems that everyone knows everyone else.

Behind all this is some pretty decent food. Not big flavor food but big food nonetheless — spilling off the plate, dripping with gravy or tomato sauce food. Like baked lasagna for $7.50 (half-order $6), veal cutlets for $9 and a seven-ounce steak sandwich for $9.85. And a page of pizzas that start at $6 and ramp up from there. It's good, handmade pizza with the standard toppings — and lots of them.

Service is brisk and friendly at the Starlite. Even if they don't know you when you get there, they will by the time you leave. It's just that kind of place.

Steeps

880 – 16 Avenue SW (Mount Royal Village)

Urban Teahouse

TELEPHONE
209-0076

HOURS
Monday – Thursday
9 AM – 11 PM
Friday
9 AM – 12 AM
Saturday
10 AM – 12 AM
Sunday
10 AM – 11 PM

RESERVATIONS
Not accepted

BEVERAGES
Nonalcoholic only

CARDS
Visa, MasterCard,
American Express,
Diners Club, Debit

Nonsmoking
Takeout

Tea was predicted to be one of the hot trends of the new millennium a few years ago, but it's had a hard go of it. I think that's because most of the tea marketers want to run either a frilly potpourri teahouse or a new age tisane joint.

But the owners of Steeps have landed on the Urban Teahouse concept with both feet. The place looks like a Starbucks (with a few more antiques), smells of high quality tea and has a lively, friendly feel. They also know how to make a decent cup of tea, whether it's the South African rooibus, peppermint gunpowder, chai masala or just a good Darjeeling.

There are light lunches available at Steeps too. For $7 you get a good bowl of soup and a house-made sandwich; add $2.50 for a pot of tea. And there are all-day sweets, from some of Calgary's better bakeries, to create your own afternoon tea party.

Stranger's

2650 – 36 Street SE

Caribbean

TELEPHONE
248-4012

HOURS
Monday – Thursday
10 AM – 8 PM
Friday & Saturday
10 AM – 9 PM

RESERVATIONS
Accepted

BEVERAGES
Fully licensed

CARDS
Visa, MasterCard, Debit

Nonsmoking
Takeout, delivery &
catering

From the outside, there is little indication that Stranger's is a Caribbean restaurant. It's in a nondescript strip mall in an area of town not known for having many restaurants of any kind. But once inside, it is obvious that this is not only Caribbean, but that it is a very good Caribbean restaurant.

I tried a combo plate of brown chicken and jerk chicken for a very reasonable $8.50. The brown chicken has a rich, mild flavor with none of the typical jerk burn. The jerk itself is pretty low on the spice-meter—they've kept it mild but have a potent hot sauce you can add for more zip. And the rice and peas served on the side are excellent.

Stranger's also does the full range of curries, baked goods and drinks that come with Island cuisine and handle the specialty of salt cod and ackee very well. The service here is also quite good—friendly and laid back in the true Island style.

Sun Chiu Kee

1423 Centre Street N

Chinese (Cantonese)

TELEPHONE
230-8890

HOURS
Sunday – Thursday
10:30 AM – 12:30 AM
Friday & Saturday
10:30 AM – 2 AM

RESERVATIONS
Accepted

CARDS
Visa, MasterCard, Diners
Club, Debit

BEVERAGES
Beer only

Monday – Thursday
Designated smoking
area
Friday – Sunday
Nonsmoking
Takeout

One of the better Asian markets in Calgary is the Lambda on Centre Street just north of the bridge. It's a great place for sesame oil, bean sauces, live eels and turtles, and all the other ingredients needed for Asian cooking. And if you get hungry just looking at all that food, there is a large restaurant attached called the Sun Chiu Kee.

Sun Chiu Kee is a Cantonese noodle house with a barbecue specialty. There are at least 133 noodle dishes on the menu from the simple bean sprout fried noodles to snow cabbage and shredded duck with handmade noodles to black bean sauce spare ribs fried Ho Fan.

As well as the noodles, you'll find numerous rice dishes, the currently trendy bubble drinks and even some Japanese and Thai dishes plus the lengthy barbecue list.

Service is very fast. If you know what you want you can be in and out in under 15 minutes. And you'll not likely have spent more than $10.

Sushi Yoko

1623 Centre Street N (Landmark Centre)

Japanese

TELEPHONE
230-1516

HOURS
Monday – Saturday
11:30 AM – 10 PM
Sunday
11:30 AM – 9 PM

RESERVATIONS
Accepted

BEVERAGES
Beer & sake

CARDS
Visa, MasterCard,
American Express, Debit

Nonsmoking
Takeout

A few years ago, the Landmark Centre replaced another landmark of my youth—the Beacon Hotel. Not that it was any sort of cultural beacon, but it did stand out on the corner of Centre Street and 16 Avenue.

Up on the second floor, Sushi Yoko sits quietly among the brightly colorful shops. The plastic food display and the short curtain are the only indications of a restaurant inside.

And a nice little place it is, with windows looking onto 16 Avenue, a few rows of tables and a couple of tatami rooms. The staff carry food out to the regulars quickly and with a smile. Yoko offers a popular lunch combo including two choices of items such as tempura, gyoza, sushi and teriyaki squid plumped up with soup, salad and rice for $7.50. The sushi slices are a bit thin, but for that price they are more than adequate. And all round, the food is fresh and tasty.

Taiwan Chili

314 – 10 Street NW

Chinese (Taiwanese)

TELEPHONE
283-6388

HOURS
Monday – Saturday
11 AM – 11 PM
Sunday
2 PM – 11 PM

RESERVATIONS
Accepted

BEVERAGES
Beer only

CARDS
MasterCard, American
Express, Diners Club,
Debit

Nonsmoking
Takeout, delivery &
catering

Tucked into a small strip mall on the east side of 10 Street NW is a tiny Taiwanese cafe known as the Taiwan Chili. With sixteen seats, it definitely qualifies as a hole-in-the-wall.

They serve the Taiwanese style of Chinese food, which is largely a blend of all the regional cuisines of China. So lemongrass and satay sauces from the south are used along with northern chilis, western curries and eastern seafood and vegetables. They even include some Japanese and Korean dishes.

The Taiwan's food is not particularly elegant; the sauces are strong and the meats are cut with plenty of bone and fat in them. But the chicken curry is a simple, forceful dish, and the sweet and sour pork is a gentle rendition.

The service is fast, the food is cheap and the staff are very helpful. You may get an earful of blaring Asian radio, but you'll also get a bellyful of reasonably good food for a great price.

Taj Mahal

4816 Macleod Trail S

Indian (Punjabi)

TELEPHONE
243-6362

WEB SITE
www.tajmahalcalgary.com

HOURS
Daily 11:30 AM – 2 PM
Monday – Thursday
5 PM – 11 PM
Friday & Saturday
5 PM – midnight
Sunday
5 PM – 9 PM

RESERVATIONS
Accepted

BEVERAGES
Fully licensed

CARDS
Visa, MasterCard,
American Express,
Diners Club, Debit

Nonsmoking section
Takeout, delivery &
catering

Founded in 1973, the Taj Mahal is the oldest Indian restaurant in the city. That's amazing longevity for any restaurant, let alone one with an awkward location on Macleod Trail and a windowless basement dining room. But the Taj has gained a lengthy list of fans over the years for its solid Punjabi cuisine.

Although dinner at the Taj can creep beyond our budget (except on Monday evenings, when a buffet is set out for $12), the lunch buffet is the way to go for a bargain. At only $10 I don't see how they can make much money, especially considering the appetites that normally pack the place.

The lunch buffet offers nice variety with tandoori chicken (they are proud to say that they were the first to bring the tandoor to Calgary), lamb korma, beef samosas, curried soy nuggets, vegetable pakoras, a number of salads and a constantly refilled bowl of naan. Service is brisk and so is the spice level, making the Taj a tangy lunch stop with big food at a little price.

Taketomi Village

920 – 36 Street NE

Japanese

TELEPHONE
207-8608

HOURS
Daily 11:30 AM – 3 PM;
5 PM – 10 PM
RESERVATIONS
Accepted

BEVERAGES
Fully licensed

CARDS
Visa, Debit

Nonsmoking
Takeout & delivery

Taketomi Village may be the only restaurant in this book to rival the Indonesia for a high quality, high value lunch. The little Japanese cafe across 36 Street from the Peter Lougheed Hospital offers some of the best food for the price in Calgary.

At lunch you can choose three items from the following: sushi (six pieces), gyoza (plain or spicy), chicken karaage, croquettes, yakitori, pork katsu and teriyaki chicken, beef or salmon. That's right, choose three of these, and they'll be packed into a bento box with some salad and rice and served with a bowl of miso soup. All for $6.75. Try to find a better deal.

And these are not skimpy servings either—or cheap sauces. The sushi is well cut, and the salmon teriyaki is a large and well-prepared piece. It's quality work and nicely presented in a lovely room.

Dinner can get pricier, especially in the sushi/sashimi area, but throughout the day Taketomi Village continues to offer excellent value.

Triple O's

10 Chaparral Drive SE

8 MacKenzie Towne Avenue SE

Hamburgers

TELEPHONE
Chaparral Drive
256-8909
MacKenzie Towne
Avenue
257-8934

HOURS
Daily 8 AM – 9 PM

RESERVATIONS
Not accepted

BEVERAGES
Nonalcoholic only

CARDS
Visa, MasterCard, Debit

Nonsmoking
Takeout

This one is for all those poor lost souls who grew up on Triple O burgers in the lower mainland of British Columbia—those to whom just the words *White Spot* bring a tear to the eye.

For the uninitiated, the White Spot is an old-style drive-in restaurant that originated in BC. They did the burger and fries and shake thing throughout the '50s and so on. But only recently have they crossed the Rockies to set up shop in Alberta. And in an unlikely alliance too.

The two Calgary White Spots are in Mac's Convenience stores in Chaparral and MacKenzie, two of the southernmost neighborhoods. The new stores have integrated small cafes that have become instantly populated with new fans of the Triple O. Maybe it's the "famous" sauce, maybe it's the history, maybe it's just the thrill of lunching in a Mac's, but the Triple O is a big—and cheap—hit. And it's not a bad burger.

Trong-Khanh

1115 Centre Street N

Vietnamese

TELEPHONE
230-2408

HOURS
Daily 11 AM – 9 PM

RESERVATIONS
Recommended

BEVERAGES
Fully licensed

CARDS
Visa, MasterCard, Debit

Nonsmoking
Takeout

Long before Vietnamese noodle shops became all the rage, the Trong-Khanh was serving big bowls of steaming bun and even larger bowls of fragrant soups. Back then you could just show up at lunch time and eat to your heart's content in the glow of the pop cooler. And you might spend $5.

These days, the Trong-Khanh has enlarged, spiffed up the place and gotten a new pop cooler. (Note to old-timers: you likely won't get locked in the biffies by wonky locks anymore.) And the bun is just as good. But you'd better make a reservation if you want to have lunch here now. It's packed every day and maybe, just maybe, you can spend $10. But only if you indulge in some of the better salad and spring rolls in the city. Or go for the lemongrass chicken or satay shrimp.

Service has always been brisk and friendly, and their popularity has not spoiled them. Trong-Khanh deserves its success.

Urban Pizza

675 Acadia Drive SE

Pizza

TELEPHONE
271-1181

HOURS
Closed July & August
Monday – Thursday
11 AM – 1 PM
Friday
12 PM – 2 PM
Tuesday & Wednesday
4 PM – 9:30 PM
Thursday
4 PM – 11 PM
Friday
3:30 PM – 12 AM
Saturday
4 PM – 11 PM
Sunday
4 PM – 9 PM

RESERVATIONS
Not accepted

BEVERAGES
Fully licensed
(Pending at press time)

CARDS
Visa, MasterCard,
American Express, Debit

Nonsmoking
Takeout & delivery

In my quest for a good quality, thin-crust pizza joint with interesting toppings, I somehow managed to overlook one that is surprisingly close to where I live. I drive by Urban Pizza a couple of times a week and have been impressed with the lineup of teenagers almost any day at lunch. But for some reason, I had not tried the pizza until the day when we had the nieces and nephews over.

We ordered a big whack of the usual pizzas—Hawaiian, bacon and mushroom, vegetarian. We were impressed with the overall quality of toppings and the crust, which was thick and tasty.

But they also threw in a couple of small sample pizzas, one of which was the Santa Monica, with red peppers, cheddar and Spolumbo's sundried tomato chicken sausage. Cooked on a thinner crust, it was excellent, full of flavor and nicely balanced.

Small pizzas start at $6 with discounts for additional pies. It's nice to see a strong independent place that knows how to make a good pizza.

Viet Nam

227 – 12 Avenue SE

Vietnamese

TELEPHONE
263-0995

HOURS
Monday – Thursday
11 AM – 11 PM
Friday & Saturday
11 AM – 12 AM
Sunday
11 AM – 10 PM

RESERVATIONS
Recommended

BEVERAGES
Fully licensed

CARDS
Visa, MasterCard,
American Express, Debit

Nonsmoking
Takeout
Patio

When it comes to Vietnamese food, no one has been around longer than the simply named Viet Nam. They bounced around in a couple of locations before settling in the upper confines of a building near the Stampede grounds. It's a dim, charmless place that has thankfully gone nonsmoking since January 2002.

The major asset of the Viet Nam is its deck, an elevated platform shaded under umbrellas that has a nice view of the urban side of the city. It is an excellent place to escape the downtown crush and an exotic refuge from the thronging crowds heading to the grounds during Stampede.

The menu is somewhat broader than the typical noodle shop. It includes lamb curry on a French loaf, deep-fried quail and lean beef in boiling vinegar—a type of fondue—as well as the popular noodles and rolls. The food is okay and fairly priced but not exceptional. But it does taste better on a sunny day on the deck.

Virginia's Palette

620 – 12 Avenue SW

*Contemporary
Mediterranean*

TELEPHONE
514-8122

HOURS
Monday – Saturday
8 AM – 5 PM

RESERVATIONS
Accepted for groups of
6 or more

BEVERAGES
Fully licensed
(Pending at press time)

CARDS
Visa, MasterCard, Debit

Nonsmoking
Takeout & catering

Virginia's Palette reminds me of the breakfast rooms found in many European hotels. It's small and cozy with brick walls, sunny tables and a short breakfast and lunch menu. The restaurant is located on the ground floor of the Lorraine Block, and the setting fits the menu well.

An open kitchen fills the center of the room. Fresh baking rolls out of the oven, while panini is grilled in one area and fruit is chopped in another. The menu moves from a vegetable frittata and roasted garlic soup to smoked salmon and marinated eggplant panini and tiramisu. It's a blend of contemporary Mediterranean cuisine and some down-home prairie treats. Virginia makes a mean butter tart.

The eggs Benedict is a hot item here, served with smoked bacon and a big pile of hashbrowns for $8. And you can eat lightly with a continental breakfast at $5, including coffee.

The setting is friendly and casual with piles of newspapers and a big table set up for larger groups. I almost feel like I should wash my dishes when I leave.

Wayne's Bagels

328 – 10 Street NW

Bagels

TELEPHONE
270-7090

HOURS
Monday – Thursday
7 AM – 6 PM
Friday & Saturday
8 AM – 6 PM
Sunday
8 AM – 6 PM

RESERVATIONS
Not accepted

BEVERAGES
Nonalcoholic only

CARDS
Cash only

Nonsmoking
Takeout, delivery &
catering

There are only a couple of places in Calgary where true Montreal-style bagel lovers buy their bagels. Wayne's is one of them. The bagels are hand-rolled, boiled and then baked in a wood burning oven just like they do in la Belle Province. And they are darned good.

Wayne has gotten a bit more esoteric with his bagels lately. In addition to the poppyseed and sesame seed traditionals, he now does blueberry, cinnamon raisin, cranberry and orange, and sundried tomato and herb. Regular bagels are 55¢ each; premiums are 65¢.

For those who want to dine in, there's a short list of egg salad, lox, Montreal smoked meat and a few other ingredients stuffed into the bagels for under $6. There are daily specials, soups and some breakfast dishes, matzo bagels, bagel chips and a variety of cream cheeses. It's not grand cuisine, but as a bonus there is always the smoky-yeasty scent of fresh bagels in the air.

Wild Sage

200 Barclay Parade SW (Eau Claire Market)

Regional Gourmet

TELEPHONE
234-9191

HOURS
Monday – Friday
10 AM – 9 PM
Sunday
12 PM – 6 PM

RESERVATIONS
Not accepted

BEVERAGES
Nonalcoholic only

CARDS
Visa, MasterCard,
American Express,
Diners Club, Debit

Nonsmoking
Takeout, delivery &
catering

Chef Dany Lamote has been involved in many of the better contemporary restaurants around town, places such as Divino, The River Cafe, Teatro, Mescalero, Cilantro and The Ranche—all fine places that are just a touch too pricey to be included in this book.

But in 2001, Lamote decided to open his own place, a tiny bay in the Eau Claire market with a handful of tables. It's a showcase for his ideas of quick, tasty food to eat in or take home and noted for high quality local and organic ingredients. Where else can you find a handmade beet-horseradish spread or a rhubarb-raisin chutney? And for a quick lunch in the Eau Claire area, the sandwiches are unbeatable.

The sandwiches—layers of spit-roasted lamb or beef on Manuel Latruwe breads with aged cheddar and a horseradish mayo—are tasty, drippy meals. And for between $8 and $9, they are excellent value. Pastas edge just over $10 as do some other dishes, but the prices are surprisingly low for the quality.

Willy's

347 Southland Drive SE

3916 Macleod Trail S

3545 – 32 Avenue NE

Hamburgers

TELEPHONE
Southland Drive
271-2888
Macleod Trail
243-1175
32 Avenue
291-6611

HOURS
Sunday – Wednesday
6 AM – 9 PM
Thursday – Saturday
6 AM – 10 PM
(Hours may vary at
individual locations)

RESERVATIONS
Not accepted

BEVERAGES
Nonalcoholic only

CARDS
Visa, MasterCard,
American Express, Debit

Nonsmoking
Takeout
Outdoor tables

On Wednesday evenings the usually brisk traffic along Macleod Trail slows down around the Willy's hamburger stand. It's Show and Shine night, and antique cars pack the lot and line up under the long canopy. It has the look of *American Graffiti* with dozens of auto aficionados comparing notes while scarfing down some of Willy's burgers.

Willy's has capitalized on the '50s burger stand look of their Macleod Trail location to generate a market niche for themselves. But even with a lack of antique cars, the other two Willy's do a brisk business with their burgers and shakes. Fans feel that the burgers taste more like those of their childhood—a time-locked hybrid somewhere between the backyard barbecue and the contemporary fast food joints.

The Macleod outlet is also one of the last of a dying breed—the drive-in that has car hop service. Even if your car is new, they will serve you as you sit in the air-conditioned comfort of your own vehicle—a dream of decades past.

Yodeling Sausage

Corner of Stephen Avenue & Centre Street S

2222 – 16 Avenue NE (Crossroads Market)

7640 Blackfoot Trail SE (Heritage Flea Market)

Sausage

TELEPHONE
No phone

HOURS
Variable

RESERVATIONS
Not accepted

BEVERAGES
Nonalcoholic only

CARDS
Cash only

Nonsmoking
Takeout

If the weather is even half decent there will be a cluster of downtown office workers around the corner of Centre Street and Stephen Avenue Walk at lunchtime. Some will be lined up at a little rolling sausage kiosk while others will be standing, sitting or strolling nearby while chomping on their favorite sausage on a bun from the Yodeling Sausage.

The Yodeling Sausage has a simple formula: good quality German sausage, mustard, sauerkraut and a decent bun, all wrapped in a napkin and served hot. It's quick, not too messy (the sausage is inserted lengthwise to prevent unnecessary spills) and cheap. It's not the least bit pretentious, and, if you're a sausage fan, you'll appreciate the simple pleasure of the presentation.

The Yodeling Sausage is also a favorite of the Crossroads Market and Heritage Flea Market and has been known to pop up in other locations. It is on wheels after all.

Zyng Noodlery

16061 Macleod Trail SE

Asian noodles

TELEPHONE
720-1963

WEB SITE
www.zyng.com

HOURS
Sunday – Wednesday
11 AM – 9 PM
Thursday – Saturday
11 AM – 10 PM

RESERVATIONS
Accepted

BEVERAGES
Fully licensed
(Pending at press time)

CARDS
Visa, MasterCard, Diners
Club, Debit

Nonsmoking
Takeout
Patio

Fast food is changing for the better. At Zyng you can get a decent bowl of noodles for a good price in a pleasant setting in pretty quick time. The small eastern Canadian chain has opened its first Calgary location in Shawnessy, and it has become instantly busy for the above-mentioned reasons.

You'll find Asian noodles in abundance — udon, Shanghai, Cantonese, soba and more. These are served with fresh vegetables and grilled meats and sauces, including teriyaki, black bean, peanut and Madras curry. They also do teas, dumplings and a disjointed collection of cheesecakes.

The sauces can be somewhat monotone and the noodles can be (inexcusably) over-cooked, but the effort is sincere and the surroundings are comfortable. Noodle bowls range from $5 – $9 with the pricier items being those cheesecakes at about $5. Dessert can also be a bit of east meets west with chocolate-dipped lychees. And the selection of green teas is quite good.

Index
Restaurants by Theme